Year 4

We are
a Team

Christine de Marcellus Vollmer
Carlos Beltramo Alvarez

GRACEWING

Authors:

Christine de Marcellus Vollmer
(Venezuela - USA)
President, Alliance for the Family
President, Latin American Alliance for the
Family (ALAFA)
Member, Pontifical Academy for Life
Member, Pontifical Council for the Family
Member, Academic Council for Values Education,
University of Carabobo (Venezuela)

Carlos Beltramo Alvarez
(Argentina)
BA in Philosophy at UPAEP and a member of the
Centre of Bioethics at UPAEP (Mexico)
Visiting Professor at the University of La Sabana
(Colombia) Family Institute, University of San Pablo
Family and Marriage Institute (Peru), and the
University of La Gran Colombia (Colombia)

First published in Spanish in 2006 by
Alianza Latinoamericana para la Familia en el Perú (ALAFA Perú) as *Somos un gran equipo* (student book three of the series *Aprendiendo a Querer*)

This English language edition first published in the European Union 2009

Gracewing
2 Southern Avenue, Leominster
Herefordshire, HR6 0QF
United Kingdom
www.gracewing.co.uk

This edition © 2009 Gracewing Publishing

The right of Christine de Marcellus Vollmer and Carlos Beltramo Álvarez
to be identified as the authors of this work has been asserted in accordance with the
Copyright, Designs and Patents Act 1988.

Illustrated by Paul Yanque

ISBN 978 0 85244 702 4

Printed by
Grafiche Flaminia - Italy

Contents

Contents

Contents

Books in this Series

UNIT
I

Understanding Sport

Objectives

*   To learn how games and sport have been played throughout history in all countries of the world

*   To understand what makes a sport: its rules and team positions, role of captain, need for practice.

*   To value sport as a means to have fun and grow in both body and character.

*   To apply what you learn in sport to the rest of your life.

Chapter 1

Sport and Why We Like It

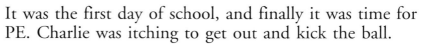

For an athlete, each move is important.

It's a challenge, a personal challenge.

Sports are organised games that test our personal skills and our ability as team players.

It was the first day of school, and finally it was time for PE. Charlie was itching to get out and kick the ball.

Mr Sullivan, the PE teacher, asked the students to sit in a circle before they started.

"Do you like outdoor games?" he asked.

"YEEEEES," sounded a chorus of voices.

"What about sport? Do you all like sport?"

"YEEEEES," the children chorused again.

"Well, I'm glad to hear that because we're going to do a lot of sport this year. Now, have you ever thought why you like them both?" Mr Sullivan asked.

There was silence and everybody looked at each other, giggling.

"Well, how about that!" Mr Sullivan chuckled. "You come here, willing to run around until you're exhausted, trying your hardest... but you don't know why?" He looked at a sea of puzzled faces.

"This year we're going to learn a lot about sport, and why our bodies (and our brains!) need it. You'll find out that sport helps you grow physically and also as a person. This is perhaps the most important thing that you will do at school: learn to be good sportsmen—and sportswomen of course. Understand? Now, another question: which do you prefer, games or sport?

A short pause was broken by Joe. "There's no difference," he said.

"There is actually a difference," returned Mr Sullivan.

"It's true that all sports are games, but they are more organised. You can have a game at break-time, kicking a ball about. During PE the game may be similar but it has more rules. To improve at a sport you have to train your body, learn discipline and push yourself. The different sports each have their own rules which are known to lots of people and they need teamwork."

"Uh-oh" said Joe, "Sounds like we are going to need brains for this."

"OK !" said Charlie. "To win a game, we need to train, but we also have to plan our tactics."

"You're right," said Mr Sullivan. "That is why sport helps develop your brain and your character, as well as your body. This year we will learn a lot about sport—its history, the lives of some famous sportsmen, different types of sports and, of course, their rules."

"All that?" sighed Joe.

"Well, you want to be good athletes, don't you?" replied Mr Sullivan.

"YEEEES!" everyone shouted together.

"OK, then," said the teacher. "For our next class, I want you to look up some piece of information, anything that interests you, about sport. Then we will talk about it in the next class." He took a ball and organised them into a couple of football teams. Everyone had a good time, especially Charlie.

"This is all right," he thought. "I hope that school is going to go on like this!"

Sport helps develop the muscles and the brain.

Good sportsmen know how to concentrate and how to push themselves.

That's why the Romans said: "Mens sana in corpore sano" (which means "A healthy mind in a healthy body".)

Sport is fun because it feels good to develop our bodily skills and to win.

That's why all over the world people enjoy sport.

1. Hurray for sport!

After reading the first lesson of our story, look for words and actions which show the good that comes from sport.

Re-order the syllables of the words listed on the stairs. Write them correctly on the steps in between.

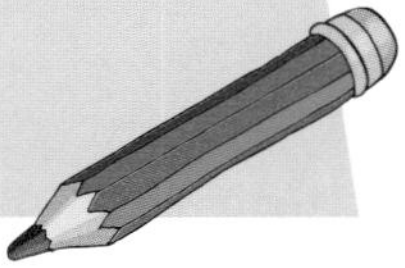

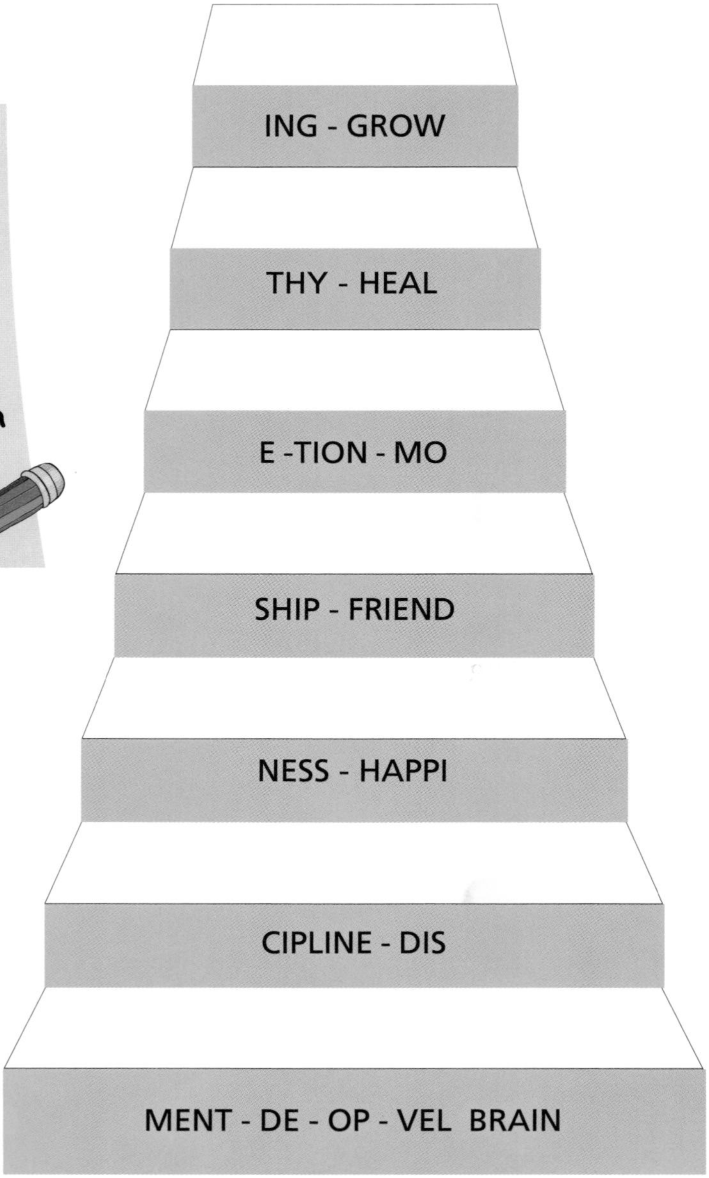

ING - GROW

THY - HEAL

E -TION - MO

SHIP - FRIEND

NESS - HAPPI

CIPLINE - DIS

MENT - DE - OP - VEL BRAIN

2. Having the right attitude

Look at the illustrations and cross out those attitudes that DO NOT help teamwork.

Happiness

Cheating

Anger

Friendship

Sadness

Effort

Based on what you have read, tell your father, mother or an adult at home about why sport is good for us.

Together make a list of ten good things about sport.

☺ It was easy

😐 It was a little difficult

☹ We need to do it again

Signature of a parent or responsible adult.

People, Games and Sport

"Do you think Mr Sullivan meant it?" Charlie asked Joe and Alice after class. "I mean, that sport is the most important thing we're going to learn at school—what about maths, and things like that?"

Mr Stevens, the Headteacher, happened to hear them as he walked past. "Mr Sullivan made a good point, Charlie," he said. "You know, sport has always been important—right back to the earliest times—in forming a person's character. Of course it's not more important than other subjects. What it does do is provide a good foundation for all the rest."

"Sir, we have been asked to do some research for our next class," said Alice, "and I am going to look up what games are played in different parts of the world."

"Sir, I want to find out more about what Mr Sullivan said," replied Charlie, "that business about games giving us what we need to develop during each stage of life. Hey, Alice, why don't we pool our findings?

"Great!" replied Alice.

""Very good, boys and girls," said Mr Stevens, turning to leave them. "Remember to tell me what you find out— I shall be very interested to hear."

In Ancient China, people played a game called 'Ts'uh Kúh' with leather balls. Players kicked and passed the ball through a hole in a huge stone. It measured 9 feet high!

The Ancient Greeks celebrated the famous Olympic Games: races, disc throwing, and wrestling competitions. The prize was a crown made of laurel leaves. Current Olympic games take their inspiration from the old Greek games, only now there are many more competitions, and athletes are drawn from all over the world.

In the Middle Ages-600 hundred years ago-men trained for war by jousting, in which they learnt how to use the sword and spear. These rough games were governed by strict rules of chivalry following the Christian ideal.

Inside castles, there used to be a game called 'Pallacorda'. It was similar to today's tennis, but was played in very uncomfortable clothes!

The Mayan Indians of Central America had their own ball game. It was played in a courtyard between two big walls, each with a stone ring on top. The players hit the ball with their hips and tried to pass it through the rings.

Some sports aim to show off sheer physical strength.

People, Games and Sport (part II)

"I like your research, Alice," said Charlie. "Games are sort of the same all over the world, aren't they, except for details. I never realised before how many different games there are with similar types of rules. Do you want to know what I found out?"

Alice nodded eagerly.

"Well, listen to this. I found out that people function at three levels," Charlie announced. "First, there is the physical level—that's the body. Sport uses both body and brain so that they work closely together. Then there is the psychological level—that's the feelings and emotions. Sport helps us to handle these."

"Like when we feel upset because we've lost a game, but we stop ourselves getting cross or bad tempered?" interrupted Alice.

"I suppose so," answered Charlie. "But there's more. There's also the spiritual level where we develop our intelligence and our willpower. It says that's how we are able to plan strategies even before we go on to the field, and how we get our determination to win."

A baby plays alone and learns to understand space and weight, and discovers textures, shapes and smells.

As the baby grows, it plays alone without rules. The baby enjoys learning to coordinate.

"Hmm. Do we play as if we were three different people, then?" asked Alice.

"No, it doesn't work that way," replied Charlie. "We are one unit that acts together in three different ways—like a boat with a propeller, a motor, and a rudder. There are three parts but one boat. The book explains that, just as it takes all three parts working together to make the boat go, so people work at three levels in everything that they do. Sport is useful because it strengthens all three."

"That's good, Charlie!" Alice was pleased. "So people have always played sport, as I discovered, and sport isn't just fun—it really does help us learn."

"Yeah," Charlie agreed. "Shall we tell Mr Stevens that sport is so useful we don't need anything else?"

Later, the child plays with other children. At first the games have no rules, but then they become more organised.

Next come games with rules. Boys and girls play with clear goals and rules that everyone must follow.

Activities

1. Let's make lists:

Working on your own, or in pairs, list five games and five sports:

Games	Sports
....	....
....	....
....	....
....	....
....	....

Sport works at three levels:

Physical Level	Psychological Level	Spiritual Level
at which we develop strength and bodily control.	*at which we enjoy playing and want to win.*	*at which we plan our game and show team spirit.*
(The body is strengthened and physical skills are developed through training.)	(Our enjoyment increases as we learn to handle feelings and emotions.)	(Tactics and teamplay need intelligence and willpower.)

2. Answer

a) What is the difference between games and sports?

....

b) What is your favourite game? Why do you enjoy it?

....

c) With whom do you like to play that game?

....

- Explain to your parents, or an adult at home, the difference between games and sport.
- Ask them what games they played when they were young.
- Were their games the same as yours?
- How did they differ?

d) What is your favourite sport? Why do you enjoy it?

....

e) With whom do you like to play that sport?

....

3. I work with my memories and my imagination

How do babies play?	....
How do 8-year-olds play?	....
How do older children play?	....

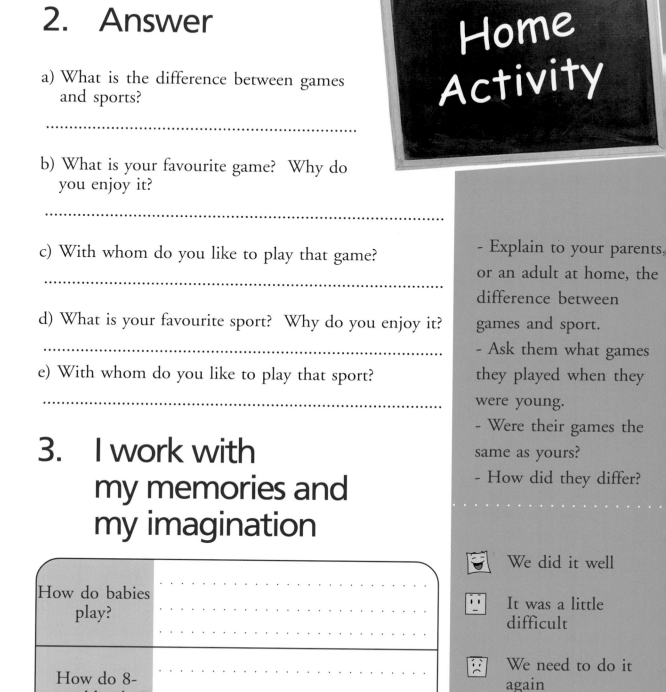 We did it well

It was a little difficult

We need to do it again

Signature of a parent or responsible adult.

Rules
of the Game

It was time for PE, and the boys were having their own game of football. They ran out of the classroom trying to see who could get to the games field first. Mr Sullivan divided them into two teams and blew the whistle for kick-off.

The game was pretty even. John, who was the goalie, sweated nervously as the ball kept coming towards him. The goal, marked by two bricks, seemed very wide. When he thought nobody was watching, he pushed the bricks a little closer together with his foot to make the goal smaller.

After a few minutes Mr Sullivan called Joe over to have a word with him. Joe returned quietly to his place but, when the ball came his way, he grabbed it with his hands, took three steps, and scored a goal.

The members of the other team protested. "This is football—you can't use your hands!"

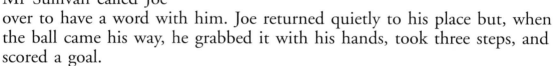

"Why not? Hands are used in rugby, and nobody objects," replied the teacher.

"But it's not allowed in football," Jamie protested.

"What Jamie is saying is that football has certain rules," said Mr Sullivan, asking them to sit for a moment. "Why are rules necessary, do you think?"

"So the game is fair for everybody?" Jamie suggested.

"That's right," said Mr Sullivan. "I asked Joe to grab the ball with his hands to show that cheating ruins the game."

John felt all eyes on him; he felt that everyone must know that he had broken the rules on purpose.

"You need to follow the rules," continued Mr Sullivan. "If you change them, then you're changing the game. Rules are there to make the game run smoothly and be fair. They mean the game is played the same by everybody everywhere. Each sport is different and has its own rules. If rules are not respected, everyone plays a different game and it becomes a mess. For instance, in rugby, netball, and cricket the ball is passed with the hands, but not in football and hockey."

"Is cheating just changing the game, then?" asked Joe.

"No, it's worse than that. Cheating lets others down," answered Mr Sullivan. "Cheats don't share the game. To cheat is selfish, and is a sign of weakness: you could even say it is cowardly."

The rules of cricket were adapted in America to become baseball.

Baseball is a game which is fun both to play and to watch. It demands many skills and great speed.

In the Olympic Games of ancient Greece, those who cheated had to put up a statue of themselves inscribed with their name and how they had cheated. These statues were known as Zanes. In 1,000 years only 13 Zanes had to be built.

19

John looked miserable but he plucked up his courage and muttered an apology. "Can we start again?" he asked. "This time I promise not to move the goal posts.

"Well done, John!" said Mr Sullivan. "I'm sure we can rely on you to respect the rules in future. But do you all think that rules only apply in sport?"

"No," said Charlie tentatively. "The other day my father complained that Paul, one of our neighbours, doesn't respect the rules. He's always parking his car in the turning space and annoying everyone."

"That's a very good example, Charlie," replied Mr Sullivan. "If a car blocks the turning space, other people are inconvenienced. You will find that there are actually many rules which we obey every day and that are really necessary if we are to live with each other in harmony."

Rugby is a game of physical contact that requires strength and speed. Rules define the game and make sure that players respect each other. Self-control is the most important rule that each player must practise. Discipline and co-ordination are essential for scoring points. Because the game is so physical, you have to learn to be humble: you will fall, but, more importantly, you will learn to get up again and to help your team-mates.

In rugby rivals are often friends. After the match there is always a "third half", a celebration for the players in both teams. Rugby started at a famous school called Rugby in Warwickshire and it attracts people willing to learn self-control while fearlessly giving their best. It needs a lot of training and team tactics, and is known to be a sport that forms leaders.

F I F A
F A I R
P L A Y

In the Football World Cup there is a special prize for the team that commits the fewest fouls. It is called the 'Fair Play' prize.

21

1. Answer:

a. Has anyone ever cheated against you? ....

b. How did you feel?

....

....

c. Have your ever cheated? Why?

....

d. How did you feel when you cheated?

....

....

2. Fill in the blanks:

My favourite game is ....

Actions allowed in this game:

1. ....

2. ....

3. ....

Actions not allowed in this game:

1. ....

2. ....

3. ....

3. Answer:

How would you feel if somebody who has cheated wins?
What would you tell that person?

....
....
....

4. What do we mean when we talk about 'the rules of a game'?

....
....
....
....

- **Tell your parents** or an adult at home what you learnt about rules today.
- Ask them why they think rules are important
Do you think that cheating and being cheated is the same thing? Why?

....
....
....

 We did it well

 It was a little difficult

 We need to do it again

. . . .

Signature of a parent or responsible adult.

Playing Your Position

Charlie was still thinking about the rules of the game as he went across to watch his cousin Alice playing rounders. He soon noticed that something was wrong. Her team had some good players and they were trying hard, but they kept losing. After a time, Miss Zeigler, their PE teacher, stopped the game and called the children together.

"Beth, what position are you playing?" she asked. "1st Deep," was the grudging response.

"Beth in 1st Deep? No wonder she's miffed," thought Alice. Beth was known to be one of the best players and 1st Deep hardly ever gets the ball.

"You know," Miss Zeigler persisted, "when you abandon your post to go into 2nd Deep, you are leaving the field open for the opponents to score."

"But I'm the best catch," said Beth, standing up for herself.

"Second Deep is not the position you're playing, though, and balls have got through where you're meant to be. Remember that all positions are important and everybody has to play where they're meant to be."

Imran wandered over to Charlie and joined him watching the match. "Last Saturday I watched a football match which was just like this," commented Charlie after a time. "One player was always playing out of position. Instead of staying at the back, he was always trying to push up-field to score all the goals."

"Yeah, I saw that game too!" said Imran. "You could tell he was a selfish player. He wasn't thinking about the team at all—he just wanted to be the big shot, scoring all the goals."

"What's up with Jodie?" interrupted Charlie. Jodie, the team captain, was limping off the field towards Miss Zeigler.

"I'm going to have to sit out," she said to the teacher as she slumped down, nursing her ankle.

"OK, let's have a look at you," answered the teacher. "We'll get someone else to take your place. Hang on. Where's Jack? He was meant to be the reserve but he hasn't shown up. Now we'll be a player short."

Jack arrived just before the game was over. He sat down next to Charlie and Imran.

"You're in trouble, Jack," remarked Charlie. "Miss Zeigler's been asking where you were."

"Oh, they don't need me," he said sulkily. "I'm just the reserve."

"It so happens Jodie hurt herself and there wasn't anybody to take her place," Imran told him.

Jack went silent. Now the game was over, the team noticed Jack on the bench. He felt uncomfortable. He knew that they had been playing hard and felt let down by him.

Coaches are responsible for helping players become the best they can. Besides knowing the moves, a good player needs physical endurance. The coach also helps develop team spirit.

Chapter 4

Jack tried to seem busy with Charlie and Imran. But Imran got to the point. "Come on, Jack. Don't dodge. You know it's no good if your team can't count on you—always. How can anyone trust you if you only do things when you feel like it?"

Jack, who always tried to look cool and make a good impression, suddenly felt very lonely and didn't know what to do. Jodie called him over.

"Come on, Jack!" she said kindly. "We need you! I'll ask to have you on my team next time if you promise you'll practise."

"Will do, Jodie!" He wasn't going to be late for another game.

In 1990, during the Football World Cup, the famous Colombian goalkeeper, René Higuita, travelled half-way down the field with the ball. When he lost it the opposition scored. Because he left his position, Colombia was knocked out.

The captain co-ordinates the team's tactics. He or she must make sure each player plays in position and plays well. The captain is responsible for the team's spirit and discipline, and for overall success.

Why do they do this? Because they know that's how they will become the best!

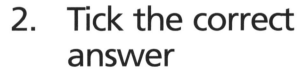

Activities

1. Reflect and respond:

a. What should Jack have done that he didn't do? And Beth?

....

b. Why was it important that Beth and Jack played their positions?
   What is the mistake each made?

....

c. Identify Beth's attitude before the teacher spoke to her. Was she a good team player, or did she harm her team by wanting to be in a more demanding position? Why?

....

d. Do you think that mistakes are useful? Why?

....

2. Tick the correct answer

a. It was important that Beth stuck to her position because...
   - O she was placed there as part of the team.
   - O the teacher said so.
   - O the captain wanted her to.

b. Jack arrived late for the game because...
   - O he was tired.
   - O he thought the team didn't need him.
   - O he didn't belong on the team.
   - O he resented being just a reserve.

c. Alice's team lost the game...
   - O because of Jack.
   - O because they didn't act as a team.
   - O only because Beth didn't stay in her position.

28

3. Alice's gossip

"Today we lost the rounders match because Beth wanted to be the star. She thinks that she's the only one who knows how to play.

And Jack didn't even show up till it was too late. It meant we were a player short. He doesn't play well, but at least he could have taken up some space on the field.

I thought I played really well. I nearly scored a rounder but nobody said well done.

Anyway, if we keep playing like this we'll never win."

Home Activity

a. What attitude does Alice show towards her team-mates? Is Alice showing team spirit?

....

....

b. Have you ever felt like Alice? What happened?

....

....

c. Do you think that every member has a contribution to make to a team? Is that important? Why?

....

....

d. What effect will Jodie's kind of attitude have? Why?

....

....

Ask your parents or an adult at home what they think about Alice's ideas. Ask if they ever felt like Alice and what they did about it?
Write down your conclusions.

....

....

....

....

🙂 We did it well

😐 It was a little difficult

🙁 We need to do it again

....
Signature of a parent or responsible adult.

The Team Captain

The next day, Miss Zeigler took the girls by themselves for a separate practice. They were still a little down because of the previous day. Miss Zeigler began by asking them what had gone wrong.

"Well, we didn't play as a team," admitted Beth.

The girls were beginning to realise how important it is to play in position. Soon they were all talking at once, asking Miss Zeigler for the position each liked best.

Miss Zeigler interrupted them. "Come on, team. You all need to learn to play in different parts of the field. Anyway, before we play, I want you to do some fitness training." The girls groaned. Running and jumping seemed like 'work'.

"I don't want to do this!" puffed Anna as she slowed to a walk.

"Why can't we practise throwing balls?" Beth whispered loudly. Several girls agreed. Jodie, however, tried to encourage the others to follow Miss Zeigler's instructions. Then one or two began to make faces and laugh at her, accusing her of being the teacher's 'pet'.

Miss Zeigler decided to call a halt. "Girls, we have a problem, don't we?" she said. "Each of you wants to play and train in your own way. Look at Jodie. Probably all of you wish you were team captain. That's quite normal and I hope all of you get to be captain at some point. But can you see why I chose Jodie? Think about what it means to be a team captain. It's not only a privilege: it's also a responsibility and means extra work. What does the captain have to do?"

A silence followed, which was eventually broken by Beth. "She has to get here before everybody else, she has to stay until the end, and she can never be absent."

"Good!" said Miss Zeigler. "What else? Julie?"

"She has to make sure that there are balls to play with and put them away at the end."

"What else, Anna?"

"She has to know how each of us plays, and help you decide whom to put where."

"Very good! Jodie, what do you have to say?"

"I think that the most difficult thing is having to keep encouraging people and make them follow the rules. It takes a lot of patience."

The Oxford and Cambridge boat race takes place every year. In 1899, Cambridge decided to carry an extra man to look ahead and give directions to the oarsmen. The tactic was so successful that rowing teams have had a 'cox' ever since.

31

"That's true, isn't it, everyone? Sometimes it's easier to obey than to give the orders. That leads to another point. Captains obviously have to learn to give instructions so that people want to obey them. But they also need to know how to follow orders themselves. You can't give instructions effectively unless you know how to obey them!"

Many people think that the best coach of all time was an American called Knute Rockne. He didn't just know his players' weight and speed: he knew how they all thought and felt and how to make the most of each person. This made him a superb tactician. His instructions were always exact but given in an encouraging way. Having been a player who followed orders closely, he knew how to give them and how to win.

In the army, those chosen to give orders are the ones who follow them best. Soldiers perform difficult, boring, and sometimes dangerous tasks. They do this because they respect their officers.

Giving orders is not easy. You need to be sure of what needs to be done, how it should be organised and how to be fair, without asking more than people can give. This will motivate others to trust you and follow your orders.

33

1.   What are Jodie's...

...responsibilities as the captain of the rounders team?

....

What do you think are the responsibilities of a team captain during a hiking expedition?

....

Imagine that you are a team captain. What do you think would be your most difficult task?

....

2.   Re-read...

... Knute Rockne's story and answer:

a. Why was it important that Knute Rockne learnt to follow orders from his coach when he was a player?

....

....

b. Why did his team win when he was a coach?

....

....

c. Why did his team trust him?

....

....

3. Team captain

a. When you are given an instruction, what motivates you to follow it?

....

....

b. What puts you off or makes you want to rebel?

....

....

c. What do you think is the best way to give orders? Why?

....

....

d. Which orders do you find the most difficult to follow?

....

....

4. Little by little towards a goal

Choose an order from your list given at 3d. above and see if you can make yourself follow it all this week. Start by filling in the form below:

Goal

I, ... , promise this week to follow a difficult order from.................. ....when he/she asks me to.. .

Think and talk about the following with your parents or an adult at home:

a) What does it mean to be a 'leader'?

....

....

b) List the qualities of a leader.

....

....

....

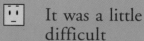 We did it well

 It was a little difficult

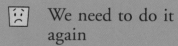 We need to do it again

Signature of a parent or responsible adult.

Competing Against Myself

"Everybody, Miss Zeigler can't coach us in the afternoons any more," said Jodie, as she entered the classroom.

Everyone looked up with disbelief and began protesting.

"So, who's taking us?" asked Alice.

"You'll never guess—it's Mr Sullivan!" Jodie exclaimed jubilantly.

At his first session with them, Mr Sullivan got all the children round him. He asked them how they were getting on.

"We almost always lose, Mr Sullivan!" complained Jack. "It makes us feel like giving up."

Mr Sullivan nodded understandingly.

> "You win when you learn to overcome your own weaknesses. That's the only way to improve."

"Do you know what is the most important thing in any sport?" he asked. "It's effort. Really making an effort. Now, tell me: in any game, who is always your first opponent?"

The children didn't hesitate: "The other team!" they answered together.

"Well, it's true that you're competing against the other team, but even before you compete against them you are actually competing against yourself." There was silence as the children thought about this. Mr Sullivan went on: "If you can't control yourself, and act as a team together, you will never conquer others. But if you can conquer yourself, and learn to improve a little bit each time, then the victories will come, I promise you."

He sat down on the grass with them.

"I'll tell you about something that happened at the Olympic Games. In 1908 the Olympics were held in London, and it was decided to hold the first modern Marathon, a long distance running race. I'm sure you've heard of Marathons. You may not know that Marathons are still officially just over 26 miles long because in 1908 that was the distance between the Royal Box in the Olympic Stadium and Windsor Castle, where the runners set out.

Anyway, that year 56 athletes competed but only 27 finished. An Italian, called Dorando Pietri, was the very first to enter the stadium, which is where the finishing line was. But Pietri made a mistake: instead of turning left, he turned right. When he realised what had happened, he fell to the ground, exhausted. People helped him up and he carried on, falling four more times. In spite of being exhausted he didn't give up, and at last he reached the finishing line. He didn't win, but the Queen gave him a special gold cup."

"That's amazing!" said Jack. "How did he carry on when he was so tired?"

"He was able to do it because he wouldn't give up. He was tempted to, but he managed to get the better of himself and of his tiredness," replied Mr Sullivan. "The gold cup was a prize for his willpower, for his ability to overcome his disappointment, and for running to the end.

"Other people's speed and excellence help us because they motivate us to improve".

— YANQUE —

Wouldn't you like to learn to be like him?" insisted Mr Sullivan. "I think you can overcome a few obstacles, don't you? What do you say?"

"How are we going to become like Pietri?" somebody asked.

"There is only one answer, and that is to learn every day to become a little more disciplined," explained Mr Sullivan. "Discipline is what makes it possible to keep improving."

"Discipline?" asked Jack.

"Yes, discipline," answered Mr Sullivan. "You can call it self-control. It's what allows us to get things done in the right order, at the right time, and in the right way, especially when we don't feel like it. You find it in every part of life. For example, we need to organise our time so that there are set times to work and study, and other times to eat, to rest and to have fun. Discipline in sport means training regularly—not just sometimes—and playing your position on the team as well as you can. That's how we continue improving."

"Sir, does that mean that, if we are disciplined, we are bound to win, then?" asked Alice.

"It also depends on acting well as a team, and on who the other team is!" replied Mr Sullivan. "But if you keep trying, you will begin winning. I suggest that you each think about what you find hardest to do in rounders, and make an extra effort to practise that particular skill."

One person who helped Pietri get to the finishing line was the journalist Arthur Conan Doyle, later famous for his Sherlock Holmes detective stories.

"I need to practise hitting the ball," said Jack, "I always miss."

"I need to learn to catch!" put in Mariel.

At the heart of the Olympic Movement is honourable athletic competition and respect for winners and losers alike.

The Olympic Games bring people together to compete fairly.

"What is essential in life is not to win, but to compete. Success is not measured by the victory but by the effort put in." (Pierre de Coubertin)

'Faster, Higher, Stronger' is the Olympic motto. It summarises the athletic ideal of achievement through effort.

1. Olympic Motto

"The effort is more important than the prize"

Explain the Olympic Motto in your own words.

....

Where can you apply this motto to yourself?

....

2. Tick the correct statement

Who is the better athlete:

O the one who tries to improve even if he or she doesn't succeed right away?

O the one who does everything just right and does not try to improve?

Why? ....

....

3. Find phrases to complete the boxes

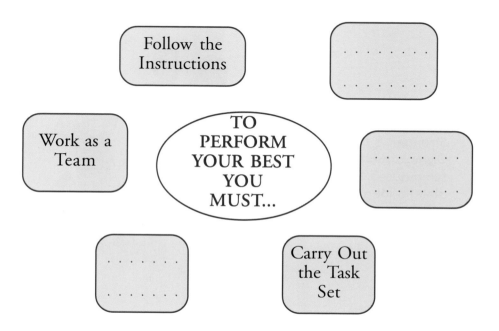

4. Create a story

Imagine that you are Dorando Pietri and you want to tell your grandson about how you finished that famous marathon.

Answer the questions:

Grandson: Grandpa, why was it so important to you to finish the race, even though you were tired and you had taken the wrong turn?

Answer: ....

....

....

Grandson: But Grandpa, if you knew you weren't going to win why did you make such an effort to reach the finishing line?

Answer: ....

....

....

Grandson: Why did the Queen give you a gold cup, Grandpa? Who did you really beat in that race?

Answer: ....

....

....

Ask your parents or an adult at home to tell you about a family mishap. Make sure they tell you how they solved the problem.

....

....

....

....

....

....

 We did it well

It was a little difficult

We need to do it again

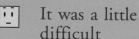
Signature of a parent or responsible adult.

Chapter 7

Growing
Through Sport

Charlie had just come out of PE, where he and his classmates had been doing exercises. They were all in good spirits except for Nick, who was upset because he found the exercises difficult. "It's all right for you, but it's no fun for me!" he complained to Charlie.

"Nick, what's going on?" asked Mr Sullivan, coming up to them both.

"I can't do the exercises," replied Nick, his eyes welling with tears.

"It's just a matter of practice," Mr Sullivan said encouragingly. "We can all develop good skills and strong muscles if we try. Some people find it more difficult, but for them, if they exert themselves, they win twice over.

"And I'll tell you something else," Mr Sullivan continued. "When you learn how to do a particular exercise, two things happen. The first happens in your brain: your co-ordination improves. The second is in your muscles: they grow. Your brain and your muscles respond in a similar way—both will only grow if you challenge them. And your spirit of self-improvement also grows, of course. That's why, when an exercise is difficult, it's really worth the effort! Remember, we all grow at our own pace, and there are things that are difficult for all of us, not just for you. But don't stop

Playing a musical instrument helps develop the neurons in our brains and the connections between them. Violinists and guitarists develop one side of their brains more than the other. This is usually the right side, which controls the left hand.

pushing yourself—and you'll see how you will improve."

"If you want, Nick, we can practise together," suggested Charlie.

"That would be great," replied Nick. "Thanks, Charlie!"

Charlie and Nick practised the exercises together for several days. Nick began to get the hang of them. Every day he was gaining in confidence—he could feel that he was getting control over his body—and he enjoyed the classes more. After several weeks of practice, Nick was finally able to do some of the exercises quite well.

"Hey, Sir, do you know that I have forced myself to practise by telling myself that every day my brain works better?" he said one day to Mr Sullivan.

"That's the way it works," smiled Mr Sullivan. "Your brain is already better organised, so your muscles respond better. Although you still find some exercises difficult, you should be very happy to know that with all this practice you are developing the health and skills of your brain as well as your body. And you have also discovered that you have the courage to overcome difficulties."

Activities that connect the axons in your brain are physical exercise, playing music, learning games of concentration and any manual skills.

You can learn anything if you practise with care and persistence

"Practice makes perfect" means that, if we are prepared to exert ourselves, we can improve at anything.

Doctors recommend exercise because it promotes good health and prevents illnesses of the body and of the mind.

43

Our brain has neurons with connectors, like 'wires', called axons.

When we perform new exercises, we build more connectors. That's how the brain develops.

These axons are useful in many other functions.

Developing them makes us more intelligent. Sport helps to develop our emotions and our mental abilities as well as our physical ones.

My PE class

1. Complete the sentences using the following words:

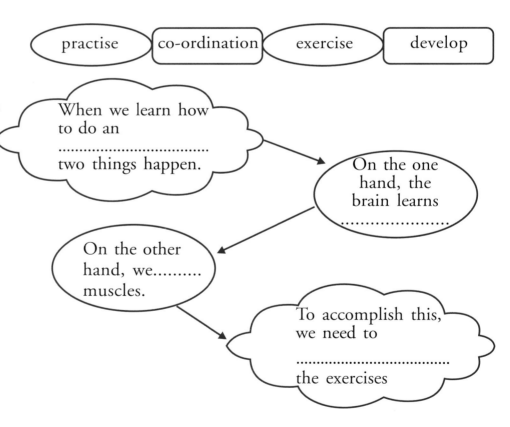

practise | co-ordination | exercise | develop

When we learn how to do an
....
two things happen.

On the one hand, the brain learns
....

On the other hand, we..........
muscles.

To accomplish this, we need to
....
the exercises

2. Think and answer

Home Activity

a. How many PE classes do you have at school every week?

....

....

b. Which activity do you like best?

....

....

Tell your parents or an adult at home what you learnt today about the importance of physical exercise.

c. Do you play a sport after school? Which one?

....

....

d. Do you like music? Do you play an instrument or sing in a choir? Would you like to?

Which instrument/s?

....

....

e. Do you do any other activity that you enjoy? What?

....

....

....

 We did it well

 It was a little difficult

 We need to do it again

Signature of a parent or responsible adult.

Chapter 8

Good Athletes

"Sir, I've heard that to be a good athlete you have to develop good work habits," said Alice, trying to sound important.

"Well, yes, Alice," replied Mr Sullivan, smiling at her.

"But what are good work habits?" asked Alice, showing that she didn't actually understand a thing.

"A habit," explained Mr Sullivan, "is something done repeatedly until you can do it easily, almost without thinking. It becomes a part of your life and how you behave. For example, in sport, when you train regularly and make a steady effort, you develop a good work habit. Good athletes are punctual, work hard, concentrate on what they're doing, and are good team-mates. And most of all, they're persevering. Like Kelly Holmes. Or Tiger Woods. Or Jackie Robinson. Have you ever heard of him?"

"No." There was an expectant silence.

"He was a baseballer in America. Baseball is the most popular sport in the US, like football is over here. In fact, Robinson was the first African-American to play in their Major League. That was in 1947. In those days, right up until the 1960s, African Americans and European Americans lived their lives largely apart. So it was quite something for an African American to join the top league.

"At first, everybody was mean to Robinson. But the manager—who had brought him on to the team—told him that the only way to get accepted was to keep his cool and to play his best baseball. So, Robinson persevered: he trained very hard, he always tried to help his team-mates, and he was never disrespectful towards his opponents, even when they insulted him. He didn't

During their active years, athletes develop very important values, such as discipline, strength, and speed. They have an enormous desire to improve. They work and live as a team, and they learn to help their team-mates.

The Nottingham iceskaters, Jayne Torvill and Christopher Dean, trained so hard that they won 12 perfect sixes for their dance routine at the Winter Olympics of 1984.

They were such perfectionists that, when they were practising, they used to make exact measurements of their tracks with a ruler.

get angry when he lost, and he never cheated. Robinson was such a good sportsman that he soon won everybody over and became one of the League heroes. In fact he received the 'Player of the Year' award in his first season. And then, because they admired Robinson, other Major League teams opened their ranks and soon a player's race no longer mattered."

"What a good story, Mr Sullivan!" said Jack enthusiastically.

"Yes. Well, of course Robinson was a fine player. But he is also remembered for his exceptional behaviour. That is why he made history as a great man as well as a great athlete."

The Romanian gymnast, Nadia Comaneci, was only 15 years old when she competed at the1976 Olympic Games in Montreal. She was the first person in history to obtain a perfect 10 for her routine. She always said that it was strict discipline which led her to perfection. It needed a lot of effort, daily exercise, and enthusiasm.

47

Word search

1. Good habits which strengthen our character are called 'virtues'. In the following list, circle the virtues needed to be a good sportsman:

Respectful - Calm - Disobedient - Persevering - Lazy - Organised - Disciplined - Disorganised - Obedient - Punctual

2. See if you can find the words you have selected in the box below.

O	D	I	S	C	I	P	L	I	N	E	D	O
B	R	E	S	P	E	C	T	F	U	L	X	B
E	P	D	I	S	O	B	E	D	I	E	N	T
D	U	P	E	R	S	E	V	E	R	I	N	G
I	N	L	Z	S	T	U	M	A	W	Q	R	I
E	C	A	X	Z	L	P	N	M	L	P	T	M
N	T	Z	Q	U	I	L	O	Y	U	P	Y	N
T	U	Y	T	O	R	G	A	N	I	S	E	D
S	A	C	A	L	M	N	L	Z	P	O	U	E
B	L	I	S	O	R	G	A	N	I	Z	E	D

3. Choose one of the athletes from the examples given in this chapter and say which virtues he or she shows us:

....

....

....

4. Choose three virtues from Exercise 1 which would help you in sport:

....

....

....

How could these same habits help you in other areas of life?

Example:

1. Being organised with my homework.

2. ....
   ....

3. ....
   ....

4. ....
   ....

Unit Self-Evaluation

Talk to your parents or an adult at home and fill in the following together.

What part of the unit did I enjoy most? ....
....
....
....

The most important thing I learnt was:

....
....
....

I should like to think further about:

....
....
....

My target area for improvement is:

....
....
....

Signature of a parent or responsible adult.

For the Parents or Responsible Adult

I will help .... in ....
....
....

UNIT II

Learning to Win

Objectives

* To learn the importance of each individual to the team.

* To encourage pupils to contribute positively in all group situations.

* To understand that effort and goodwill are more important than the number of successes scored.

* To realise that strength of character is built through consistent effort.

Chapter 9

Defeated, but Undaunted

Excitement was running high as Charlie's football team got ready for a match against a neighbouring school. Charlie's grandfather was there, next to his parents.

Most of the players were listening to the referee's final instructions. But Charlie's mind had wandered back to Jackie Robinson, the baseball player. All the children had been talking about him. "I wonder how he felt in his first League game?" he asked himself. "I wonder if he was nervous—"

The great player is not the one who never falls, but the one who gets up again right away!

"Did you hear what I said, Charlie?" boomed the Ref.

"Yeah, sure," said Charlie, caught off guard—but in fact he had not been paying attention and had missed everything.

He ran down to his position in goal. The ball was far away and his mind drifted off again. He was imagining that he was playing alongside Robinson. In fact, he was just as famous himself. Whoosh! The ball left Josh's boot and tore past Charlie, who was completely unprepared. It was the silliest goal that he had ever let in!

After that, Charlie was on edge for the rest of the game. He felt so ashamed and wanted to get off the field as quickly as possible.

His team lost, 1-0.

"It was all my fault that we lost," he said. "I don't want to play any more, Dad."

"I know how you feel," replied his dad. "But you have to get back in the saddle—and the sooner the better!"

"What saddle, Dad?" frowned his son.

"After a fall, you need to get right back in the saddle again."

"It's an old saying," explained his father. "It comes from horse-riding. It means that, if you're afraid and don't face up to your fear, the fear will get worse. So it's better to face up to it immediately."

"Yeah, that makes sense," said Charlie.

"Listen, Charlie," his dad continued. "We all have weaknesses to overcome. Yours is day-dreaming; for someone else it might be impatience, or lack of co-ordination, or laziness. But the worst weakness of all is wanting to quit when we fail, and that's what you have to work on now."

Charlie thought about it. Wasn't one of Jackie Robinson's best qualities to go on in spite of setbacks?

His own first challenge was to turn up at practice the next day. What were his team-mates going to say after that really embarrassing goal? Some of them were actually wondering if he'd dare show up—but he did.

And he went straight up to Mr Sullivan. "Sir, I'm sorry that I wasn't paying attention yesterday. I shouldn't have let that goal in," he muttered in everybody's hearing. "But please let me stay as goalie. I want to try again and do better next time."

Mr Sullivan smiled at him. That was just the attitude he wanted from his players.

1. Let's help a friend

Let's help a friend find out the steps they need to take to overcome some difficulty.

Example: Peter is good at maths, but he always gets bad marks in spelling. What should he do?

- Find out which words he normally spells wrongly.
- Write each word 3 times.
- Ask somebody to check his spelling until he gets the words right.

a. Dane always gets told off because he shouts when he speaks. Should he shrug it off, telling himself that that's his way of speaking, and continue being told off? Or should he do something about it?

....

....

....

In the past, travelling was possible only by horseback, and horses are not always easy to ride. People used to fall and had to face getting back on the horse again. The longer it takes us to do something difficult, the more difficult it becomes.

b. Olivia is always late for school. How could she correct this?

....

....

....

c. Nathan sends the ball wide every time he bowls. Should he give up cricket?

....

....

....

d. Rose always forgets to take her gym shoes to school on Fridays.

What steps could she take to help her remember?

....

....

....

2. Thinking back

a. Have you ever felt like Charlie? What triggered the situation?

....

....

....

b. What mistake did you make?

....

....

....

c. How should you have behaved?

....

....

....

Ask your parents or an adult at home what the following means to them:

"After a fall, you need to get back in the saddle again."

Write down a few conclusions.

....

....

How can we get over our bad experiences?

....

....

....

....

It was easy

It was a little difficult

We need to do it again

....

Signature of a parent or

Knowing My True Worth

"You want to be a better goalkeeper, do you, Charlie?" Mr Sullivan asked.

"Yes, Sir," Charlie replied.

"Well, you'll have to learn from Maya," Mr Sullivan said. Charlie looked across to a small girl running for

the ball. She was the smallest on the field. "She used not to be on the team because she's so small. But she desperately wanted to play and spent the whole summer practising. When the team selection came round at the beginning of term, she got in."

"But I don't see her scoring any goals," Charlie pointed out after watching her for a while.

"True. But do you notice how alert she is, always ready to be where the ball is?"

Charlie watched a little more.

"Each mistake that we make can teach us how to do better."

"Maya keeps improving her game, and even though she is tinier than some of you others, she is quicker and more precise," Mr Sullivan remarked.

"You're right," said Charlie surprised. "She doesn't look that impressive, but did you see that, Sir? She knows just where to send the ball... making it easier for her team-mates."

"Let me tell you something that my father would always say to me," Mr Sullivan said. "'Look at your weaknesses because under them lie some of your strengths.'"

"What does that mean, Sir?" Charlie asked.

"Look. Your particular weakness is that you're a dreamer... but it's also your strength. Dreamers can make many of the things they dream about come true. But day-dreaming at the wrong times—like yesterday, during the game—may lead you to failure. So, it's good to be a dreamer, but not during an exam, or when you cross the road! At those times you need to be completely alert, don't you?" Charlie smiled. "And then," Mr Sullivan continued, "it's not enough to dream; you must work hard if you are to be the best. You, young man, need to train harder and concentrate more."

There is a champion rugby team whose Latin motto is "IN HUMILITATIS VINCIT" meaning "Humility makes us winners."

57

"Mr Sullivan seems to know me quite well," thought Charlie guiltily.

"We all need to find out what our weaknesses are and then work at them," Mr Sullivan said kindly. "But it's also important to identify our strengths and build on them too. You, Charlie, can contribute a lot to the team. How about starting to train a little more every day? I can give you an exercise routine. Then it's up to you."

"Look at your weaknesses: that's where your strengths are hidden."

Each person has double-edged characteristics which are both strengths and weaknesses depending upon how they are developed and used. Some common ones are:

Being patient

Being impatient

Being tolerant

Being a dreamer

Being very precise

Being a good listener

Learning from others

Being ambitious

Being tall

Being short

Being aggressive

Having quick reactions

Having slow reactions

Being thoughtful

Being lively

Some characteristics help one to succeed in spite of occasional defeats:

Having the humility to recognise one's own weaknesses

Having the determination to go on despite everything

Being able to work hard

Being courageous

Knowing how and when to ask for advice

Being aware of difficulties

Enjoying the success of others

Being punctual

Developing good routines

In netball the tallest players have the advantage of height, but the shorter ones can be quicker and more agile.

1. Connect the phrases

Each one of our double-edged characteristics can develop either into a weakness or into a virtue depending upon how we choose to act.

Virtue	Characteristic	Weakness
I dream of big things that I would like to do, and I prepare to do them.	Determined	I help my friends but not my family.
I force myself to excel at what I do, and I insist that others do what they have promised to do.	Outgoing and popular	I spend all day fantasising about the future, and don't pay enough attention to the moment.
I am helpful and cooperative with everyone.	Imaginative	I want my own way and I don't listen to others.
I can make people laugh and have a good time.	Humorous	All I do is joke around and don't take anything seriously.

2. Complete the table

Home Activity

Choose 4 characteristics that can be good or bad and complete the table below, indicating when they are a virtue and when a defect. (Do not choose the ones used in Activity 1.)

Characteristic	Good	Bad
. . . .		
. . . .		
. . . .		
. . . .		

The Big Winner!

Charlie and his dad went that Saturday to watch the county Youth Team play. To their surprise, they saw Mr Sullivan. He told them that he had come to watch his nephew Andy who was playing in the match.

Throughout the game, Charlie found his eyes glued to Andy, who was clearly one of the best players. He knew how to get the ball, but he rarely kept it to himself for long. He was there supporting his team-mates, passing it to them so that they could score. In fact, he only scored one goal himself, but he had set up several. Charlie was particularly impressed to see that, when Andy's team eventually won, he was able to celebrate without doing down the other side or making them feel small.

"Andy's amazing, Sir!" Charlie exclaimed afterwards.

"Yes, he is, isn't he?" answered Mr Sullivan proudly. "But you know, he wasn't always. His secret is that he's never big-headed. He

Humility's Virtuous Circle

- Having the courage to analyze my game
- Recognizing my weaknesses
- Working to correct my weaknesses
- Improving my game
- Gaining self-confidence
- Throwing myself into the game with more energy and daring

has great humility, on and off the pitch. Would you like to come across and meet him?"

Charlie couldn't believe his luck. "Yes! I certainly would," he replied enthusiastically.

"Hello, Uncle!" Andy said, coming towards them. "Great to see you here! So this is Charlie? My uncle says that you're one of his best goalies!"

"Well, I can't play like you," replied Charlie, embarrassed. "You were terrific!"

"Thank you," Andy answered with a warm smile. "But I never found being a goalkeeper easy. It's hard work keeping alert, especially when the ball appears to be far away, and then suddenly it's there, in the goal, and you get blamed for letting it in! Actually, I have always found I learn most when things go wrong." He laughed again. "But you have to be prepared to admit your mistakes, don't you Uncle? Do you remember that awful match against Whitchurch?"

They began wandering off the field. Andy was greeted by his mates as he left. "It's a great experience playing for a really good team," he said. "It's worth all the hard work and the training, and the regular meals and sleep. I bet Uncle has told you that there are no short cuts, and he's right."

Andy seemed to be able to talk while also slapping his friends on the back: "Great game, Jock!" "What a goal, Tim!"

He turned to Charlie again. "When you do well, it's easy to think you know it all and are better than everyone else. As soon as you start thinking that you stop learning. And, however good you are, you can always get better still!"

"Wow, Dad! Why does a champion like Andy think that he has to improve?" Charlie asked, after Andy and Mr Sullivan had left them. "I bet he'll go all the way to the World Cup!" His dad smiled. Charlie continued,

In the finals of the 1950 Football World Cup, Uruguay played against a strong Brazilian team, who only needed a draw to win the cup. To the surprise of the 174,000 spectators, Brazil was overconfident and Uruguay won 2-1. This event is known as 'the Maracanazo' after the famous stadium in Rio de Janeiro where they played.

"But, Dad, you know what? The thing I like best about him is how he treats everybody. Do you think all champions are like him?"

"Perhaps not all, Charlie," his dad replied. "But in general, the best athletes are kind and generous to their team-mates and also to their opponents. You must have heard the term 'being a good sport'—that's what it comes from. And now it's time you and I were getting back to the house or Mum will be asking what's happened to us."

Humility gives us courage because it takes away our fear of failure.

Good tactics and close co-operation make for good play and success.

Failures always provide us with opportunities to learn and improve.

65

1. Re-read the text and answer:

– What impressed Charlie most about Andy?

....

....

....

– Did those attitudes help his team?

....

....

....

2. Complete the sentence:

The virtues of a good winner are:

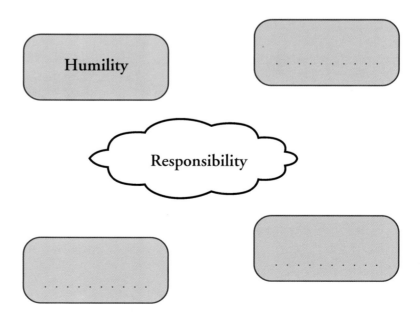

Humility

Responsibility

. . . .

. . . .

. . . .

3. Make sentences

Make sentences with the virtues listed above to show why each is important.

a. ....

b. ....

c. ....

d. ....

e. ....

4. Complete the Vicious Circle

Turn back to the Virtuous Circle at the beginning of the chapter. Can you make a contrasting Vicious Circle for being arrogant?

Vicious Cycle: being arrogant

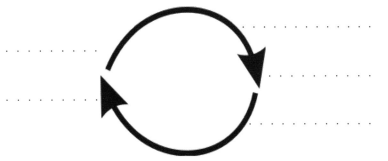

Choose from the list below to make further Vicious Circles:

Being defensive	Giving up
Not open to advice	Blaming others
Rejecting criticism	Feeling inadequate
Being a pessimist	Lacking spirit of improvement

Together with your parents or an adult at home analyse Andy's remark:

"As soon as you start thinking that you know it all, you stop learning.

That's when you begin to lose."

Conclusion:

....

....

....

....

 It was easy

It was a little difficult

We need to do it again

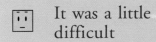

The Poor Loser

'Arrogance' is thinking oneself the best, and not seeing the talent in others. Arrogant people don't want to see their flaws, because they don't want to admit that others may be better still.

Charlie and his dad were on their way out of the stadium where they had watched Andy's match. Suddenly they heard angry shouts. Charlie turned and saw three players from the team which had just lost. One of them was very upset and was arguing with the others.

"We lost because nobody would listen to me!" he was yelling. "I reckon I'm the only one round here who knows how to play football!"

"What's he so cross about?" Charlie asked his dad. "I didn't notice him playing very well. I never even saw him pass the ball—he kept it himself until he lost it."

Charlie felt that the player's attitude was letting down his team. He asked Andy about the argument when they caught up with him in the crowd.

"He always behaves like that when he loses," said Andy. "He hogged the ball on the field, but he didn't score one goal. Now he wants to blame the others for losing."

"You mean he's always more interested in his own game than in helping his team win? And now he's angry because he didn't score a goal and the team lost too?" asked Charlie.

"Yup, that's it!" Andy replied, "His name is Oscar. He was one of my team-mates last year. He's got talent, but he used to miss a lot of practices.He thinks he's the best because he is big and quick, but in fact he causes problems. He can get the ball all right, but he's no team player. In fact we lost a lot of matches because he used to fight with everyone, including the referee. It's a pity, because he could be brilliant. If he doesn't look out he'll lose his place on this team too."

Charlie looked back at Oscar, who was still shrieking at his team-mates. "It's impossible to play with you guys!" he was shouting.

Andy heard him too. "He really should watch it. He's played for three different teams in the last couple of years," Andy continued. "He's got skill but he's such a bad sport. He wants everyone to think that he's the best—the trouble is, he's not."

"Yeah, I wouldn't want him on my team," Charlie agreed.

For all that, Charlie had really enjoyed going to the match and was excited about his conversation with Andy. He told his friends all about it the following Monday, and made a point of going up to speak to Mr Sullivan after football practice.

"Sir, how do we make sure that the team has got the

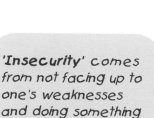

Poor losers have little capacity for self-criticism, and they don't want to see their own mistakes. We call them 'insecure'. Insecure people tend to blame others for the mistakes they make.

'Insecurity' comes from not facing up to one's weaknesses and doing something about them.

69

right attitude in the Football Tournament next week?" he asked.

Mr Sullivan looked Charlie in the eye. "Don't you worry about the team," he said. "Just think about your own attitude. Then you'll find that things will turn out all right."

Vicious Cycle

Self-criticism is the capacity to see and understand our own good and bad actions.

Confidence does not win without skill. Skill without confidence is unreliable. Skill and confidence together make for success.

We gain in courage and humility when we are able to continue with confidence in spite of difficulties.

Two Enemies of Success are:

Being overconfident

Being defeatist

1. Let's Help Charlie

Charlie has got all the labels mixed up, and now he doesn't know where each belongs. Can you help him?

Arrogant   Helpful

Fair   Generous

Never shares   Envious

Humble   Kind

Grumpy   Cowardly

Responsible   Disciplined

A bad loser is...

· ·
· ·
· ·
· ·
· ·

A poor loser is...

· ·
· ·
· ·
· ·
· ·

Making our best effort + analysing our progress + facing our weaknesses = self-confidence.

People who are arrogant and don't make an effort are heading for failure.

2. Think and answer

Tell a story about a time when you lost a game.

....
....
....
....

Do you think you took losing well? Why?

....
....
....

Give an example of a bad loser.

....
....
....

How do you think he/she should have taken it?

....
....
....

Re-read with your parents or an adult at home the information shown along the sides of the story.
Write down any ideas you think are important.

....
....
....
....

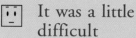 It was easy

It was a little difficult

We need to do it again

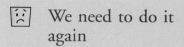

Signature of a parent or responsible adult.

Chapter 13

The Losing Team

Everyone was enthusiastic about the Football Tournament which was to begin the following week. Mr Klein offered to give Charlie's team an extra coaching session. Charlie himself practised every day. He wanted to be on top form so that he wouldn't disgrace himself in goal again.

During the 1990 World Cup in Italy, Cameroon's team surprised footballers by leading against England 2-1. Then, in the second half of the game, the African team lost confidence and wasted many opportunities, losing 3-2.

However, when they discovered that their first match was to be against one of the strongest sides their hearts sank.

"We are sure to lose!" Joe said pessimistically to his friends.

"I don't know why we're even trying," complained Nick. "They're much better than we are!"

Charlie didn't like this talk. "Of course we can beat them if we try!" he encouraged them. "Anyway, it's just the first game. Whether or not we win, we can learn from it and see how we're doing. Come on! Let's make an effort."

Everyone was very nervous when the match began. They started to fight for the ball and forgot to pass it. In fact, they forgot to play as a team at all.

"I told you to pass to me!" shouted Imran.

"But I had a chance to score a goal!" Joe retorted.

"I was closer to the goal than you!" complained Imran.

"Stop arguing and start playing," snapped Nick.

The game was a disaster. They lost three-nil and at the end no one said a word.

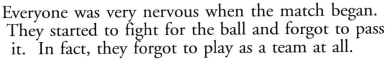

The next day, Mr Klein spoke to them before their practice.

"Well, team. Why do you think you lost?" he asked.

"Because the other team was better," Imran muttered sullenly.

"Because we fought each other instead of playing the other side," said Charlie. "We weren't focused."

It is always easy to criticise others. But, through constructive self-criticism, we can improve each day and gain self confidence. Confidence is based on knowing that we have made our best effort to prepare ourselves

"I agree with you, Charlie," nodded Mr Klein. "You didn't act as a team. Do you think it's fair to say that you were defeatist, assuming that you were going to lose instead of getting in on the attack?" Mr Klein looked round the group. "Fear of losing can make you lose," he said. "You didn't lose just because the others were better—to some extent you all brought the loss on yourselves. You will find that, in a team, failure belongs to everyone just as much as success does.

"Now, cheer up," he continued, seeing their long faces. "What would you say to some training from a member of the County team?"

"Is it Andy?" called a chorus of voices as with renewed enthusiasm they ran out on to the field.

The Battle of Waterloo, fought in Belgium in 1815, marked a turning point in history. Napoleon Bonaparte, Emperor of France, had already conquered most of Europe. His army was the largest yet assembled, and he thought he could easily beat the English, too. He became overconfident.

The Duke of Wellington in a famous victory had a much smaller army but he paid attention to detail. He used the lie of the land to fool Napoleon into thinking he had more men. In addition, he took great care of the safety of his soldiers.

Activities

1. Circle:

Circle the phrase below which you think best describes the topic of this chapter.

a. The importance of optimism (a positive attitude).

b. The effects of pessimism (a negative attitude).

c. Teamwork.

2. Complete:

Complete the sentences below by writing down what happens when someone in a group is pessimistic.

a. If a team believes that it can't win, and they don't make an effort because they are afraid of looking ridiculous, then

....

b. If one of the players acts selfishly by keeping the ball instead of passing it, then

....

c. If a defender leaves his position to try to score a goal, then

....

d. If a player loses control and begins to push others, then

....

e. If a player is lazy and doesn't care if the team wins, then

....

f. If the captain wants to be the star and doesn't pass the ball to anybody else, then

....

g. If the members of a team compete among themselves by fighting for the ball and pushing each other, then

....

....

h. If someone kicks the ball hard without caring where it will go, then

....

i. If a player stumps off screaming, "I'm not going to play anymore—you're all cheats!" then

....

3. Reflect and respond:

a. What did Mr Klein mean when he said, "You didn't act as a team?"

....

....

....

....

....

b. The negative attitudes that harmed Charlie' team were:

....

....

....

....

Team Spirit

"Let's go!" shouted Andy, who joined them at the next practice. "Come on team!"

At first, the children tried to show off. They had the same attitude that they had shown during the recent match. They pushed each other and fought for the ball, and they all tried to catch Andy's attention.

After a few minutes, Andy stopped the game.

"Look, each of you is trying really hard and I can see a lot of talent here," he told them. "But what about some teamwork? If you want to win, you're going to have to learn to play well yourselves and to pull together as a team. For example, George and Sally—you're meant to be playing midfield. Think what you're doing. That's right, you should be passing the ball to Paul or Jamie, because they're the forwards."

"What about Fred and me?" interrupted Mark. "We're in defence so we can't plan what we're going to do with the ball."

"No, but you should be guessing the other team's tactics," explained Andy.

Little by little, they began to understand the importance of working together and planning their moves. Everyone contributed ideas. They practised passing, and they switched positions on the field to take advantage of each player's strengths. At last they were able to zigzag the ball all the way to the goal.

Team spirit is about...

... thinking and feeling part of a group

... working for the victory of each team member by doing what's best for the team rather than what's best for you as an individual.

... defeating laziness and the desire to 'show off'.

... feeling happy about other teams' victories.

... knowing and respecting everyone's strengths and weaknesses.

By the end of the next practice, everyone was suffering from muscle pains. They were hot and they were tired. Mr Klein suggested that they go to bed early. The tournament was coming up and they needed to get some rest.

At last the day arrived. The team entered the field for their first match feeling very fit. Their opponents had expected an easy win and were surprised by what they found. They began losing confidence while Charlie and his team-mates gained in theirs.

Concentration and discipline paid off. Charlie and his team won!

And the following week, they beat another school. They had again been nervous beforehand because they knew they were up against better players. However, their close teamwork and careful strategy gave them the victory, 1—0.

At the end of the match, the team crowded round Rachel, congratulating her for scoring the goal.

"Thanks, everybody," she said, flushed with pleasure. "But actually the goal also belongs to Paul. He passed me the ball."

"We won!" shouted Mark, jumping up and down. "All of us! We all played together, we passed to each other and we stayed in our positions."

"Excellent, Mark!" Mr Klein said. "And you're also learning to share your successes and failures. Well done, everyone—now you're really starting to show team spirit!"

Rome became the centre of a great empire because of its strong team spirit. At an early age, children learnt to be proud of being Roman and to use that confidence to give of their best.

Because sailing depends on wind and current, it requires great physical ability. It demands muscle, endurance, speed and agility. Teamwork is essential because control of the boat depends on the movements of each of the crew.

In 2002, Turkey beat South Korea to reach third place in the World Cup. The Turkish team were jubilant. Seeing the disappointment of the losers, they invited the defeated team to join in their celebrations. The spectators were so impressed that they gave them a round of applause.

The most important thing in teamwork is to believe that each member's actions affect the group's results.

1.   Connect with arrows:

Draw arrows to connect the virtues (on the left) to their definitions.

Generosity

Responsibility

Obedience

Teamwork

Doing our duty

Doing as we are told by someone in authority

Co-operating and working with others

Considering others and sacrificing for them.

2.   List the above virtues:

List the four virtues above in order of importance. Put the most important at the top, then the next most important, and so on. Work out in your head why you have put them in your chosen order. Could you explain it to someone else?

....

....

....

....

3. Virtues for winning

Home Activity

Circle the virtues of a winning team.

Camaraderie - Dislike - Discipline - Envy
- Flexibility - Perseverance - Care -
Loneliness - Endurance - Consistency - Laziness -
Generosity -Sacrifice for the group - Selfishness -
Following the game plan - Envy - Attention to detail
- Pain tolerance

Discuss with your parents or an adult at home the inset on p. 79 "Team spirit is about ...".

Together, answer: How do we have team spirit at home?

....
....
....
....
....

4. Choose two virtues:

Choose two virtues and write down actions that help you develop them.

Example:

Responsibility:
– Attending practices.
– Finishing your homework.

....
....
....

....
....
....

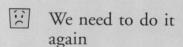 It was easy

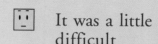 It was a little difficult

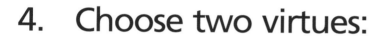 We need to do it again

. . . .
Signature of a parent or responsible adult.

Unit Self-Evaluation

I ask my parents or an adult at home to help me with this unit's self-evaluation.
Colour the house that shows what you have learnt from this unit... and write why you deserve that grade and what you need to improve.

....
....
....
....
....

Signature of a parent or responsible adult.

UNIT III

My Family is a Great Team

Objectives:

* To see the family as a team: strong, loyal, and effective.

* To understand that families look out for the well-being of all their members by having rules and special positions to play.

* To think about what you are responsible for in your family.

* To appreciate what all the others do.

My Most Important Team

The family is the group in which we begin our social life and learn how to relate to others.

Our self-confidence is formed within our family, which is where we learn to take our first steps in life.

Just as the school team was performing really well in the Football Tournament, life at home became tense. Charlie and Alice started comparing notes on the scoldings they were getting.

"Mum is upset with me," grumbled Alice. "She says that all this football means I've not been helping enough at home. I think she's going to stop me going to extra practices."

"Hmph. Your mum must have spoken to my dad," said Charlie. "He's just told me the same thing. It's tough—just when everything is going so well at school, our parents decide to make our lives miserable at home!"

Being a good team member is about...

Acknowledging others' good work and contributions.

Not leaving things lying around where others want to sit.

Helping someone with a difficult task.

'Playing your position' and doing what you are supposed to.

Turning up on time.

Being willing to take over work from someone else.

Charlie and Alice heard somebody laughing—they turned to see Mr Sullivan standing behind them. He must have overheard their conversation.

"Well," he said, coming up to them, "your parents are right. If you think about it, your family is like a team, isn't it? It's actually the most important team you'll ever belong to. The family gives us life, then it protects us and gives us happiness. Each member has a function—a position."

Alice looked puzzled.

"Yes," said Mr Sullivan, looking at them both. "A family is a team - it has a captain, it has rules, and it has members. And each member is indispensable. Now, Charlie, didn't you tell me that you always take the rubbish out at home?

It's a small task which may seem boring, but it's very important. Imagine what your kitchen would be like if nobody emptied the rubbish for a month!"

Charlie laughed. "It would be a real mess, Sir."

If a person doesn't play their part, it affects everyone.

If I keep my family commitments, my family will trust me and give me more freedom.

"It would, wouldn't it? That's why you shouldn't think that your household jobs are unimportant. Just think," Mr Sullivan continued, "if you stop doing your jobs, your mum and dad will be left with them all. And then what? Well, two things will happen, won't they? Firstly, your parents will think that you're not yet responsible, and you are not ready for more freedom. And, secondly, you will not be developing your character. And that is even more important than the rubbish and its smell, isn't it?"

Alice was thoughtful. What Mr Sullivan had said made her feel guilty. When she got home, she asked her mother if she needed any help.

"Well, it would make a big difference if you could tidy your room," her mum replied with a surprised smile.

That weekend, Alice set to work. She and her big sister Marcia tidied their room, and Alice got the younger ones putting their things away too. Meanwhile, their mum was able to get on with the washing, and another brother helped their dad repair an old dresser.

"What a difference, Alice," her mother exclaimed at the end of the day. "That was such a help. While you were doing the rooms, I've been able to wash and iron that pile of clothes." She looked about her. "Your room is so tidy you can get at the drawer to put yours away!"

Dad was pleased, too. He inspected each room, and praised the children in turn.

"Now, let's see if you can keep your rooms like this. All right, everybody? If we all make an effort, we can keep the whole house tidy, and it will make it a happier place to live in."

TOWERS

The Family Coat of Arms

A long time ago, in feudal times, warriors fought wearing armour. This made it difficult to recognise soldiers on the battlefield. To identify themselves, they began carrying a banner, and wore a light coat on top of their armour embroidered with a family symbol. The symbol came to be known as their 'coat of arms'. Castles and important belongings also displayed it. In time, all warrior families created their own coats of arms. Everyone hoped that their family would be remembered as the most courageous and honourable.

Communication is essential for the happiness of the family. To establish good communication, everybody needs to listen and be listened to.

1. Answer

Accepting Change

During our lives, we will see our family go through many different events: a relocation, a new member in the family, an unemployed parent or a sick person. It is easier to adapt to events if we face them together, as a team.

a. Do you think that Mr Sullivan exaggerated about the rubbish? Count the bin bags before answering.

....

....

b. What would happen if Charlie didn't take out the rubbish? Why?

....

....

c. How would the kitchen in Charlie's house smell? Why?

....

d. Is it important for you to be able to count on your family? Can they count on you?

....

....

e. What are the advantages of being known as someone who always does his/her part within the family team?

....

2. Think and answer:

a. Do you think that it is important to help out at home? Why?

....

....

....

....

b. How do you help to keep your house tidy?

....

....

c. Do you always do your jobs or only sometimes? Why?

....

....

With your parents or an adult at home answer the following:

a) Have your parents or an adult at home ever been angry with you for not doing your jobs?

....

....

b) Do you think they were right? Why?

....

....

....

 It was easy

 It was a little difficult

We need to do it again

. . . .

Signature of a parent or responsible adult.

Chapter 16

Captain of the Home Team

Charlie and Alice liked the idea of the family as a team. They and some of their friends were talking about the role of team leaders as they walked home after school.

"Do you think that families also have a 'coach'," asked Charlie, "you know, like Mr Sullivan?"

"Well, I know that I'm always being asked to improve!" Alice answered. "My dad is forever challenging us to do more and get better at it—he's a bit like Mr Sullivan!"

If it wasn't for our ancestors caring for their children, we wouldn't be here today. What do you know about prehistoric life?

"Yes," grinned Karen. "That's just how it is in my house too—except it's usually my mum who gives the orders. She's always wanting us to do things better and telling us how to improve," Karen said.

Ann, one of Karen's friends, added: "Well, in my house I would say it's my grandmother who's the boss. I love her a lot, but she expects so much. She never stops!"

"Would you say that your dad is the boss in your house then, Alice?" asked Karen.

"Well, I'm not sure. Sometimes it's Dad, and sometimes it is definitely Mum. But I can't imagine a family without someone in charge," Alice said. "Otherwise, everybody would do what they wanted, and nobody would take care of us and the house."

"That would be great!" Karen exclaimed.

"Would it? What if people were out for themselves and didn't get on with anything that needed doing? There wouldn't be anybody to keep order, or to tell you what's right and what's wrong,

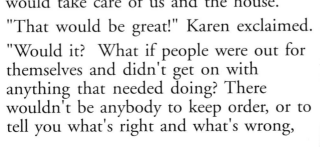

or to show you how to do things," Alice pointed out, thoughtfully. "There'd be nobody to help you or to look after you."

"I'll never forget that embarrassing goal, do you remember, when our team lost because of me," Charlie interrupted. "I felt so bad I wanted to give up football, but my dad really helped me to get over it and keep playing. And he has also helped me practise."

"And if you think about it," added Alice, "they're in charge of a lot. They have to pay the rent, they buy all our food, our clothes, the things we need for school, not to mention the heating and the electricity. We're always being told to 'turn out the light—it's expensive'. They have to work really hard to pay for everything. And then at home they have to make sure that things run smoothly, that we support each other and don't fight—you know."

"I suppose you're right," said Karen. "I just expect things to be there, but I can see that really they come from Mum and Dad's hard work—because they care for us. Jodie said the other day that to be a captain takes patience and sacrifice. Maybe it needs even more to captain a family."

"Well, everybody wants to have a family," said Charlie.

"And a family needs a good captain to work properly."

Matthew, who had said nothing so far, now joined in. "The families I know are very different from each other. But I suppose that they all have somebody who organises them and is in charge. Yeah, you're right. A family without someone in charge is not a real home."

"True," answered Charlie, "and in my house we're all happiest when the boss is happy, and Dad is happy when we behave!"

Adults take care of their families in many different ways.

Activities

Farm work is very demanding. Often the harvest needs the help of workers from other countries. These workers leave their families for as long as is necessary in order to support their families.

Many times we don't understand our parents' orders. But we need to respect and obey them because parents have good reasons and want what is best for their children.

1. Fill in:

Who is the leader of your family?

Give one or two names and say how you are related.

...........................He/she is my ....

...........................He/she is my ....

2. Answer:

Think about your family:

a. What does the leader of your family team do? Tick all his/her responsibilities.

O Pays for the house
O Buys food
O Responds to emergencies
O Takes me to the doctor
O Pays for the electricity
O Pays for the oil/gas
O Mends things that break
O Buys books
O Buys clothes
O Is in charge of me legally
O Any other responsibility? What is it?

....

....

b. Which of these things do you think are important in a family leader?

O Works hard
O Pays attention to detail
O Looks after the house
O Pays taxes Gives us tasks
O Helps with homework
O Organises family outings

O Repairs things at home
O Sets an example
O Picks you up at your friend's house
O Gives you permission to go ou
O Pays for food and heating

c. What do you enjoy doing with your family leader?

....

....

....

3.   What's going on?

Look at the pictures. What's going on? Write a short story.

....
....
....
....

....
....
....
....

....
....
....
....

....
....
....
....

Tell your parents or your 'family leader' what you learnt about leaders.
Ask them to tell you how it was when they were children.
On a separate sheet of paper, write down one of their stories.

....

....

(Find some family photographs, put them in an envelope, and bring them to school.)

It was easy

It was a little difficult

We need to do it again

....

Signature of a parent or responsible adult.

No Rules!

Alice and Charlie were going to visit Grandpa. They were late.

"Yesterday our mums said that we were old enough to help with some spring cleaning," Alice puffed in explanation. "We had so much to do, we couldn't finish it all! We had to throw away the things we don't use, give away clothes that don't fit us any more—she even got us cleaning under the beds! That's why we're late, Grandpa—sorry. Can we have a drink, please?"

Alice's tone showed she was half complaining and half proud that 'the boss' was giving her more responsibility. Grandpa smiled. "What about you, Charlie? Have you been tidying too?"

"Yeah! I had to put away my clothes, put all my toys in their boxes, and sort out my bookshelf," said Charlie, also quite pleased with himself.

"Well now, that's good," said Grandpa as he poured them out some drinks. "But aren't you always expected to put your things away? What are the house rules when it comes to your rooms?"

"Oh, I don't like rules!" Charlie responded taking a gulp. "I like doings things when I feel like it."

"Do you, now?" Grandpa replied. "But if there weren't

More than 700 years ago, in the year 1300, thousands of pilgrims arrived in Rome to celebrate a 'Holy Year' because it was the beginning of a new century. They arrived on foot, because there were no other forms of transport and only the rich had horses. There was such a crush of people that Pope Boniface VIII ordered everybody to walk on the right of the road.

any rules, how would you know who does what and what to expect?"

"Well, yeah, there are some things everybody has to do, but all the same, I still don't like rules."

Grandpa looked at Alice and Charlie thoughtfully. "Do you know," he said, "when I was young like you there were no dishwashers, so we had to wash everything up in the sink. There were no washing machines—we had to wash clothes in the sink, too. And there was no central heating, so we had to wear lots of clothes, and they all had to be washed. That added up to a lot of different jobs.

"I remember being very cross with my dad one day when he asked me to go outside and get coal for the fire. He was firm, though. He explained that, without rules, nothing would ever get done."

"Yes, Grandpa," put in Alice. "We did what we were asked yesterday, and it was quite fun, but I think that at home one has to be able to relax as well and not think about rules all the time."

"I know what you mean, Alice. Of course you need to play as well. But you'll find that everything in life has its rules and regulations. Take baking a cake, for instance," Grandpa smiled. "Just think, to bake a cake you need the right amount of ingredients—butter, sugar, flour, eggs and milk—

On horseback it was easier to ride on the left, leaving the right sword arm free against oncomers. This happened everywhere until the 1700s when the design of wagons in France and America made it easier for them to swap over. Napoleon spread this rule throughout Europe. However, wagons in Britain were different and we were never conquered by Napoleon, so in the UK we continue driving on the left even today.

and you have to cook it at the right temperature. And if you forget to take it out at the right time, it won't be much of a cake.

"People are a bit the same. If you have any number of them living or working together, you need rules just to keep things running between them smoothly and fairly."

"Like traffic rules or the rules in sports?" asked Charlie.

In Babylon, 4,000 years ago, King Hammurabi published a code of laws for his empire. It is the first known code of this type and it meant progress for justice and for his people.

"You're right, Charlie," Grandpa replied. "What would happen to traffic without rules? In a different way, music has rules, too, and because of them it has harmony. If there were no rules, it would just be a noise. But with rules one can make all sorts of music. Gymnastics, sport, everything we do has order—or it would result in a mess."

Alice looked puzzled.

"Look," said Grandpa. "Think of your family. What would happen if nobody followed the rules? If nobody picked up anything or put anything away? If Dad decided he didn't want to go to work any more; and Mum couldn't be bothered to do the housework? You'd be hungry and cold, and you'd have so little money you'd have to move—"

"Oh, I wouldn't like that," said Alice.

"No," added Charlie. "I like our house, and Mum said we're having lasagne tonight, my favourite!"

"That sounds OK to me," said Grandpa. "But you see your mum is obeying the rules. In fact she's obeying them twice over: she's obeying the rule which says you'll be hungry and she needs to feed you, and she's following the rules for making a lasagne. Everybody needs to obey rules, and they count on others following them, too. That's the way life works!"

The Ten Commandments are the rules of good social behaviour revealed to Moses on Mount Sinai 3,200 years ago. They are respected by Jews, Christians, and Muslims and form the basis of all the laws of civilisation. They protect the weak from the strong. The Ten Commandments are also known as The Decalogue.

The Magna Carta

In 1215, 800 years ago, a group of noblemen forced King John to sign a letter limiting his powers. The English 'Magna Carta' became a model for people in other countries.

1. Complete:

Complete these rules:

If you use it...   *put it away.*

If you open it...   ....

If you make a mess...   ....

If you take off your clothes....   ....

If you find it left open...   ....

If you find it left lying around... ....

If you unwrap a sweet...   ....

Napoleonic Code
In 1804, Napoleon established a new code of law in France to help reconstruct the country after a bloody revolution. It was designed to guarantee justice and allow the country to run smoothly. This 'Napoleonic Code' was adopted by all the countries of Europe which were occupied by Napoleon, and in the French colonies. It still forms the basis of law in the whole of Latin America.

2. Think...

Think about your own house rules. Can you name five?

a. ....

b. ....

c. ....

d. ....

e. ....

3. Answer:

Home Activity

a. What are the most important laws in a country?

1. ....

2. ....

3. ....

4. ....

5. ....

b. What are the most important rules for traffic?

1. ....
....

2. ....
....

3. ....
....

4. ....
....

English Law is built on an older system called Common Law. The judges say what the law laid down by Parliament (or Statute Law) means in a particular case, and the courts then have to treat other cases in a similar way. If there is no Statute Law and no earlier example to follow, the judges decide what is right and make the law themselves. Common Law became the norm throughout the British Empire, and is still used in America, Canada, and in the Commonwealth.

Talk to your parents or an adult at home and ask them why rules are important. Why are they useful? When are they necessary?

....
....

Ask them to tell you what their house rules were when they were children.

Write them on a blank sheet of paper.

 It was easy

 It was a little difficult

 We need to do it again

Signature of a parent or responsible adult.

Chapter 18

My Family, a Winning Team

The winning family learns to appreciate each of its members' contributions to its well-being and happiness.

Alice was skipping along and singing on her way home, watching her shadow jump in front of her. It was long and thin because the sun was setting behind her.

I wonder if I'll look like that when I'm older, Alice thought to herself. Would she be as tall or taller than her mum? It would be nice to be grown-up and to be free. Then she remembered what Grandpa had been saying about life always having its rules, even for grown-ups. Would she have to live with rules all her life? But then Grandpa had said life was happier with rules. What were adult rules like?

She arrived home. Dad was saying goodbye to Uncle Edward.

"Hello, Alice," Uncle Edward said. "I hope you're ready to get to work."

Alice didn't know what he meant, but her dad told her the plan. "Tomorrow it's going to be all hands on deck. We're going to clean and paint the house . Your mum and I have long wanted to get on with it, and now the rest of the family have offered to help. There's going to be a lot to do—for you children, too."

That afternoon they all went to the DIY store to choose paint and buy everything else that would be needed. There was a lot of discussion about which colours to buy. Mum wanted light colours, but Dad pointed out that they wouldn't cover up the old paint. Mum was at last persuaded and she found some colours that she liked.

The family team practises by doing small daily tasks. That's how they learn to co-operate in bigger projects.

Work began early on Saturday morning. Aunt Suzy and the men were going to do the painting. The children's job was to move the smaller furniture and put out newspaper to protect the floor. Soon they were even allowed to paint some of the walls, while the adults got on with the woodwork. Little by little the house began to change.

Meanwhile, Alice's mum got to work upstairs, making curtains ready to hang once the paint was dry.

By mid-day they were all feeling tired and hungry. The bell rang and the children leapt up to answer the door.

"Grandpa! Granny!" they called out excitedly. Their grandparents had arrived with large baskets of food. The children helped them carry it through. This is like a party, Alice thought.

By the end of the day, the house was looking wonderful. "All we need are the curtains!" Aunt Suzy remarked. "But look, you're never going to sleep here. The furniture is all over the place and the smell of paint will keep you awake. Come and spend the night with us."

What a crowd there was! Somehow space was found for each of them. Supper was created out of the remainders of lunch and what Aunt Suzy could find in the kitchen. It was another party. Even though she was dropping with tiredness, Alice felt very content. Her family really was a team—a winning team!

Activities

1. Answer:

a. What big projects has your family organised, where each member had a special part?

....

....

b. What projects would you like to do with your family team?

....

....

c. What entertainment projects, such as holidays, picnics, etc., has your family organised?

....

....

d. Acting can be fun. Have you ever taken part in a family performance at home or in a neighbour's house?

....

....

e. Do you sing or play instruments together? Have you heard of the film 'The Sound of Music?'

....

....

f. Some children have a surprise performance for their mum's birthday. Would you like to do this with your family? How would you do it?

....

....

2. Sometimes...

Sometimes we begin a project, but we don't finish it. Write down a project that you were unable to finish. Why couldn't you finish it?

Home Activity

....

....

3.   Write:

Write about a project that your family organised. Was it a success. If so, why?

....

....

....

With your parents or an adult at home, think about your answer to Activity 3. Write down anything else that you or they can remember about it.

....

....

....

....

....

In a winning family, everyone makes small sacrifices to help each other.

 It was easy

 It was a little difficult

 We need to do it again

Signature of a parent or responsible adult.

Unit Self-Evaluation

Colour the balloon that represents your performance in this unit.

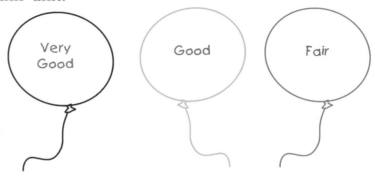

- Why do you think that you deserve that grade?

....

....

- What was difficult in this unit was

....

....

- In the next unit, I want to improve

....

....

Signature of a parent or responsible adult.

UNIT IV

My School is
Another Great Team

Objectives:

* To explain what is meant by school team spirit.

* To value your school as a team and consider yourself an important member of it.

* To encourage responsibility within the classroom and for school work.

Chapter 19

My Classroom Team

"Silence everybody. I've got something important to tell you." Mrs Mandy waited until the children settled down before she announced: " Next month the school's going to hold a Science Fair. Each form is being asked to prepare a project based on the science we have been doing. There'll be a competition involving the whole school. All your parents will come and look at the displays and the school governors will award prizes for the best projects."

A sea of hands shot into the air at this. "Miss, can I take part?" "Who's going to choose what we do?" "What about making a spaceship?" "Yeah, that's a great idea."

Mrs Mandy smiled at their enthusiasm. "The first thing is that everybody's going to take part—and have a special part to play. "Next, we've got to choose a topic. We've been studying living things this term so I thought we'd make a Botanical Garden. We're going to start by planning the display. Yes, Charlie?"

"Miss," Charlie said, "we're going to need a lot of earth as well as all the plants."

"And flowerpots to put them in," added Samantha. "And..."

"Slow down, everyone!" said Mrs Mandy. "First, let's decide what we want our garden to look like. When we've done that, we'll be able to make a proper list of the things we need and also decide who is going to do what."

"Let's be really organised so our project is the best!" said Jake.

"Yeah!" everybody shouted together.

There are different ways in which we build our community.

Some of these are:

Caring about a friend... when we show **solidarity**

Defending an innocent person...when we stand up for **fairness**

Respecting those who think differently from us... when we are **tolerant**

They decided that they needed three teams. The first team would design the garden and make a list of what they would need: plants, amount of earth, and all the other materials. The second team would create some posters describing the plants that they were going to use, and the conditions that they like to grow in. The third team would be responsible for bringing everything to school. The whole class would have a part in putting the display together.

At last it was time to start putting the garden together.

"It's going to be cool," Charlie said excitedly.

But then they noticed that something was missing. There was no earth.

"Hey, where's Mark?" Samantha called out. "He was supposed to bring the earth."

"How can we have a garden without earth?" Frankie grumbled.

Everyone was cross with Mark. Without the earth they couldn't begin building. They had done so much work, and now their display was ruined. The pots, the plants, the posters all meant nothing because one essential ingredient was absent.

The Headteacher saw them standing around and asked what had happened. Nobody said anything. They just looked miserable.

"I'm never going to trust Mark again," said Frankie to Charlie. "We're all going to be disqualified just because of him!"

"Yeah, but we don't know what actually happened to him," said Charlie. "Maybe he couldn't help it."

"I don't care!" Frankie replied. "It's all his fault."

Hmm, thought Charlie. So this is what it is to be a team at school. We're a team at home, and we're a team at school, too. We can't help depending on each other. It was really bad of Mark letting us down. Still, I can't help thinking that something must have happened to him..."

Activities

1. Class Brainstorm

Big projects are only possible when people work together and rely on each other.

Make a list of the people who are needed for the following:

Example:

> **To build an aeroplane:**
> *designer, engineers, mechanics, metalworkers, glass workers, electricians, upholsterers, electronics engineers*

To build a house:

....

To build a motorway:

....

To create a telephone system:

....

To sell a box of eggs:

....

To make a loaf of bread:

....

To travel to the Moon:

....

To create a good class atmosphere, everyone needs to: listen to each other, take turns talking, follow the teacher's instructions, and be fair to each other.

Great projects only succeed when people work together in a team, know their targets, follow a clear plan, and rely on each other.

2. Answer:

Home Activity

1. How do you feel when somebody offers to help you and remembers to do it?

....

2. How do you feel when you count on someone for help, but he/she forgets?

....

3. How do you feel when you offer to do something but then you don't do it?

....

4. How do you feel when you promise to do something and you do it, and do it well?

....

5. How do you feel when you are part of a good team? Why?

....

....

....

People need to communicate. In every society, knowledge and progress depend on how well we communicate.

With your parents or an adult at home, re-read the chapter and pick out the people who showed poor team spirit.

Write down your conclusions.

....

....

....

....

 We did it

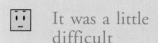 It was a little difficult

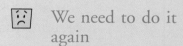 We need to do it again

. . . .

Signature of a parent or responsible adult.

Chapter 20

The Truth Will Out

Year 5 won the Science Fair with a splendid model of an illuminated solar system. They were so pleased that they jumped up and down with excitement. Then they started making fun of the other class projects, poking them and breaking bits off.

But the following Monday the situation changed. The Headteacher called some of the Year 5 students to his office. When they emerged they were looking embarrassed and angry. They were muttering to each other and saying: "It's not fair!" and "He can't do this to us!"

At Assembly, Mr Stevens addressed the whole school. "You've probably all noticed that something has been going on," he said. "So I will explain what has happened. You will all remember that Year 5 won First Prize at the Science Fair. We were all very impressed with their solar system project. I am sorry to have to say that some of the class were so excited about winning that they let themselves go. They began making fun of other people's projects, and even damaged some of the models." He looked severely across at the rows of children. Some of the Year 5 pupils began looking at their feet and shuffling them with embarrassment. "But worse than that," the Headteacher went on, "we have since discovered that they cheated."

Loud whispering broke out at this.

"They cheated," said the Headteacher raising his voice, "by copying a model from another school instead of creating their own. I want you all to know that it is dishonest to use somebody else's work and pretend that it's yours.

"These children have let down their classmates, who didn't know that their model wasn't original. They've taken an unfair advantage over students in other years. And they've let themselves down.

"You may wonder why I am taking their actions so seriously," the Head went on. "Cheating is bad not only because it lets others down and makes those who do it look foolish if they are caught out. It's bad because cheats stop themselves from learning. If they go on doing it, they can seriously upset their future."

Mr Stevens looked round at a sea of serious faces.

"Just think," he said, "Would you want a doctor to operate on you if you knew he had cheated to pass his exams instead of learning how to do his job?"

"No!" said everyone in chorus.

"What about crossing along a bridge built by an engineer who cheated instead of learning how to calculate the dimensions?"

Again there was a chorus of disapproval.

"Well then, you can see that Year 5, or those who were in on the cheating—and I don't think that that was everybody—have behaved very badly indeed. So I am forced to take strong action. I'm going to have to take their prize away."

A murmur of voices broke out again in the hall. Everybody looked at each other and started talking at once. "Well, I'm glad!" Frankie whispered to Charlie. "They were mean!"

Standing next to the Head was the Chairman of Governors. "We're all surprised at the behaviour of these students," she said seriously. "A scandal of this kind affects the whole school. However, I have discussed with Mr Stevens what action we shall take and we've agreed that, to be fair to everybody, we'll repeat the whole event after half-term."

At this, all the students started clapping and laughing.

"Everybody will be able to take part," she went on, "including the students who were disqualified."

"Excellent," thought Charlie. "We'll get a second chance too, and this time the earth will be there!"

Richard Nixon, a president of the United States, was eventually forced to resign from office because he lied

Ben Jonson, who held the 1987 100-m world record, cheated by using drugs to help him run faster. As a result, he lost all his records and titles.

Activities

Athletes who use drugs to achieve greater strength or speed take an unfair advantage over others. Cheating like this destroys sport.

1. Answer:

a. Have you ever been cheated?

....

....

....

b. How did you feel?

....

....

c. Have you ever cheated?

....

....

....

d. How did you feel?

....

....

Cheating in politics and business damages individuals and society as a whole. It is called 'corruption'. Corrupt people often begin by cheating at school.

All games must be played fairly. Playing with cheats is a waste of time and causes arguments.

114

2. Think:

a. Would you put your trust in a doctor who cheated at school? Would you prefer a doctor who had studied hard? Why?

....

....

b. What do you think when you hear that 'government funds' (money provided by your family and by the community) have been badly spent?

....

....

....

c. How does a thief think? What would you say to one?

....

....

d. How does a person who cheats think?

....

....

e. Do you think that cheats are happier than other people?

....

....

....

Talk to your parents or an adult at home about what it would be like if people cheated at home. Together, write down some of the things you think of.

....

....

....

....

☺ We did it

😐 It was a little difficult

☹ We need to do it again

. . . .

Signature of a parent or responsible adult.

Chapter 21

Making Things Happen!

Everybody at school was talking about Year 5 and how they had cheated. The Head called a parents' meeting to talk about how the families and the school might work together to improve the children's attitude.

Charlie and Alice's parents doing up Alice's house. They suggested that a large project done as a 'school team' might help. Why not invite the parents and students to redecorate some of the classrooms? The parents agreed. Many were willing to give up their time to help, and one father, who was a professional decorater, said that he would supervise the project. He and the teachers could make the plans over half-term.

The following Saturday, everyone arrived at the school early in the morning. They brought food with them so that they could take a break from painting and enjoy breakfast and lunch together. Everybody was given a job and the older students were allowed to help with the painting. With so many people working together good progress was soon being made.

Charlie and his friends chatted while they worked. They started talking about Mark.

"Has anyone found out why he didn't turn up at the Science Fair?" Charlie asked. Nobody had. Nobody had actually spoken to him since. "Don't you think we ought to ask him to explain?" Charlie insisted.

"All I know is that he didn't turn up!" said Frankie angrily. "We don't need his help this time. We don't want to be disqualified again."

"Look, we don't know why he didn't show up," interrupted Alice. "At least we should find out."

School is where...

... we get the knowledge that we'll need in the future.

... we build the world of the future.

.. we learn to work together, respect, and understand each other.

Charlie was feeling increasingly uncomfortable. He had also been cross with Mark, but he had a niggling feeling that they in turn hadn't always treated Mark fairly. At last he got up the courage to speak out.

"Well, I think that Mark might have let us down because he was cross with us. We played a nasty trick on him last week. You know—when we hid his book on the highest shelf, and then made fun of him because 'the egghead' couldn't finish his homework? We shouldn't have done that."

Nobody said anything.

"Charlie's right," said Alice. "We're always teasing Mark even though he never bothers us."

"You know what… I wouldn't like it if you did that to me," said Karen.

"Let's all go and find Mark and tell him that we're sorry," said Alice.

No-one wanted to, but they followed Alice and Charlie all the same.

When they found Mark, Charlie told him that they were all sorry for the trick that they had played on him.

"We really want you to be our friend, Mark," he said. "We were just being silly."

Mark, who was ashamed of having spoilt the class project, was surprised by their apology. He was also very pleased. Soon they were all talking about how this time their botanical garden was going to be the best.

117

My schoolmates and I are responsible for making the atmosphere at school good or bad.

Sometimes we cause problems and fight, but that only makes more problems.

Learning self-control and teamwork make us stronger all round.

1. Complete:

Complete by answering each question:

a. How should we behave if we want a school that is:

clean?

....

happy?

....

interesting?

....

beautiful?

....

fair?

....

b. How would the teachers react if we always:

paid attention?

....

greeted each other politely?

....

worked together?

....

wanted to learn?

....

....

lied?

....

....

caused problems?

....

....

2. Write below:

What does the following Golden Rule mean to you?

"Do to others as you would have them do to you."

....

....

....

We all make mistakes. Recognising our own mistakes and apologising are noble gestures. Being able to forgive other people's mistakes is twice as noble.

Home Activity

Tell your parents or an adult at home what you have learnt in class. Ask them if they have had similar problems. What do they do if they are faced with one?

....

....

....

....

 We did it

 It was a little difficult

 We need to do it again

. . . .

Signature of a parent or responsible adult.

Chapter 22

My School, a Winning Team

Two days before the second Science Fair, Year 4 had a football match against a neighbouring school.

They always enjoyed playing there because it had such a good big field.

Just as the game was about to start, it began to rain. Everybody ran into the school.

Charlie looked around. What a mess it was! Even some of the windows were broken! He and his friends looked at each other. They wrinkled their noses at the bad smell. How strange, they thought. The school was bigger than theirs and had a much better playing field. They had assumed that the building would be better than theirs too.

The bell rang. Children piled out of their classrooms, pushing and yelling.

Charlie looked at Mrs Mandy nervously. "Miss, what's the matter with this school?" he asked. "Are all these students really poor?"

"No, Charlie, but I think I know why you are saying that. The school looks poor because it's badly looked after. If you look after things well it creates a much better atmosphere, doesn't it?" answered Mrs Mandy.

"So, the school looks like this because the students don't look after it?" asked Alice.

"Yes," replied the teacher. "If you think about it, a school belongs to all the people who work and study there as well as to the people who own and run it. If you are careless and break things, your school will become a much less attractive place."

"Well, the students in this school are really careless!" said Charlie.

"Yeah," agreed Alice, "but we can't really talk. Think of all the litter which collects in our playground. It goes all over the place as soon as the wind blows."

"Yes, it's horrible then," said Mrs Mandy. "We need to do something about it."

"Do you think that these children's mums let them leave things lying around at home too?" asked Alice.

"Well," replied Mrs Mandy, "if they don't look after things here, their rooms at home are probably just as bad. Other people's mess is unattractive, isn't it? And clearing up and cleaning can be fun, especially when it is done together. We found that when we painted the classrooms. You all worked to make them look nice, and now you want to keep them clean."

The visit to the other school made the children appreciate their own one even more. On top of that, the Science Fair was now also upon them them. They all worked harder than ever to make it a success. In the end they just missed winning, but the Head praised their botanical garden highly as he gave them second prize.

Everyone went home after the Fair tired but very proud. It was good to be part of a school that was truly a winning team.

At school we learn facts and skills but we also learn to become good citizens.

Cesar Casatty, a rural Argentinean teacher who lived around 100 years ago, worked in a very poor school that had no electricity or running water. There were only two small classrooms, and students had to take turns attending classes. In spite of all the difficulties, the school's atmosphere was so pleasant that it became very successful. Students learnt to read and write, and also the many practical skills needed for life in a farming community.

121

Activities

In some private schools in America, students organise themselves into teams to clean up the school during the last 20 minutes of the day. Students enjoy this and the schools save a lot in cleaning costs.

1. Answer:

a. After reading about Charlie's neighbouring school, what does the following expression mean to you?

"We are responsible for our own world."

....

....

....

b. Why does Mrs Mandy think that the students at that school probably live in messy homes?

....

....

....

c. Who do you think is responsible for things looking nice in a school?

....

....

Some French schools ask parents to help. During the holidays, they gather for a whole week to paint and repair the school inside and out, sharing their skills.

2. Connect with an arrow:

Draw an arrow to connect the people or organisations and their responsibilities.

Teachers	Pay taxes
School Administration	Study well
Government	Support the school
Students	Run the school
Community	Teach well

3. Your opinion

Why do we have schools? Write your opinion below.

....

....

....

Unit self-evaluation

Colour the face that represents your performance in this unit.

Very good   Good   Average

Why did you draw that face? What were your contributions?

....

....

What could you or should you improve?

....

....

Signature of a parent or responsible adult.

UNIT V

My Community Team

Objectives:

* To discover that the community is like a huge team

* To understand that we all have rights and duties in our community.

* To value the laws that organise our community and ensure its security and happiness.

* To respect our elected leaders

Playing My Part

Alice and Charlie were enjoying school much more than at the beginning of the year. They felt more confident and had deepened their friendships. They were also doing well in class and in sport.

"School's fine," Alice said to Charlie, as they walked home one day, "but you know, Charlie, I get a bit scared sometimes going home. Did you hear that some houses near us have been burgled? We had some neighbours round last night, and they and Dad were talking about what they could do to make the area safer," said Alice.

"Yeah," replied Charlie. "I overheard my dad and mum discussing that as well. It makes me a bit spooked, too, especially when it's dark, but Dad told me not to worry. He explained that all the grown-ups of the area are going to create a Neighbourhood Watch scheme. He described it as

a team effort to get rid of the burglars."

"Yeah, Dad explained that to me, too," said Alice. "Everybody's going to keep an eye out for each other's houses when they're away. They're also creating a 'telephone tree' so that we're all alerted quickly if something suspicious happens. Each person has four people to ring, and those people ring four more, till everybody's been contacted. Don't you think that's a good idea?"

"Depends who's doing the ringing!" replied Charlie. "If you were on the line, you'd talk so much you'd forget calls three and four! Seriously, did you hear that they want us to take part, too? They're going to organise us into a 'kids' watch group', and train us to look out for anything strange that we might see in the park or on the streets."

"Really?" said Alice, excited and a bit scared all at the same time. "That sounds fun, but won't it be a bit dangerous?"

"Well, of course we'll have a group leader. We'll only have to keep our eyes open and report to the leader who'll know what's serious and what should be passed on," said Charlie.

"Oh!" said Alice. "Well, that sounds OK, then. It's quite a responsibility though. We don't want to make false reports—like the boy who cried 'wolf!'" Suddenly Alice stopped and started searching in her bag. "By the way, Charlie, can you help me with my maths homework? I don't understand question 2 ..."

It's always better to be with someone on the street, especially at night. You must remain alert, and avoid talking to strangers. Don't be afraid; just be careful.

In Mexico City there is a youth organisation called the 'Young People's Association Shield'. It works with the police and its main purposes are to engage young people in the prevention of petty crime and to develop community self-protection schemes. Police train its 40 instructors and five hundred children take part.

COMMUNITIES CAN BE GOOD TEAMS

Neighbourhood Watch schemes have been developed in many cities around the world. Sometimes residents take turns to watch the streets; sometimes they pay for the service. They raise the alarm in various ways which can include simple things like whistles and bells.

127

1. Answer:

a. Communities where everybody works together are more prosperous than others. Why?

....
....
....

b. Whose responsibility is it to ensure a safe and well ordered community?

....
....
....

c. How can you and your friends help in the community?

....
....
....

In America, the groups of Covered Wagons that went west were famous for their organisation. Settlers had to travel many months before finding a good place to settle. The wagon trains travelled during the day, and at night they were grouped in a circle. Women and children stayed in the centre around a fire, while men collected firewood or kept watch to warn of possible attacks by Indians. Everybody felt protected and knew their responsibilities. Men hunted buffaloes and other animals to provide meat for food. When they arrived at a river or lake, they bathed and washed their clothes. Through teamwork, these settlers were able to build a new and prosperous country.

2. Public places

Public places belong to all of us because they have been built with our taxes. Libraries, hospitals, parks, and city buildings are examples of public places. We can all use them, and we must all take care of them.

Each town is run by a Council. Complete the table by filling in the responsibilities of the Council and of its citizens.

Local Council	Citizens' Responsibilities
	To respect traffic signs.
Maintain and clean streets.	
	Use, respect, and take care of libraries, hospitals and city buildings.
Create and maintain green spaces, squares and parks.	

Talk to your parents or an adult at home. Memorise information such as your name, address, telephone number, and an emergency phone number. Make sure that you have the right information. Ask them what you should do if you are faced with a dangerous problem on the street.

 We did it

 It was a little difficult

 We need to do it again

Signature of a parent or responsible adult.

Smart? Or a Wise Guy?

Charlie was imagining that he was a policeman as he strutted along to school the next day. Rounding a corner, he found himself looking up at a real policeman talking to a group of people. There had been an accident between two cars, and an ambulance was at the scene.

One car was badly smashed. Charlie shivered when he recognised it—it was one he had seen many times driving through red lights. The police officer was telling the onlookers that this 'wise guy' of a driver had paid a high price—it was because he was jumping the light that he had hit the other car which was innocently driving through green.

"Some people are pretty stupid," he said, shaking his head. Charlie had by now been joined by some other children and the policeman came over to them.

"Now," he said, addressing them all, "take a good look at that car. The driver was in such a hurry that he thought he'd save time by jumping the lights. Instead, he's on his way to hospital, then he'll have to go to the

police station—and then he'll have to buy another car! My warning to you is that it's really important to look at the lights and obey them, even when you're just crossing the road."

Charlie was telling his classmates about the accident when George pulled him aside. He said he had forgotten to do his homework and asked Charlie to give him the answers.

"Come on, George," Charlie frowned. "That's cheating, and cheating never helps in the long run. That accident I've just told you about—it was caused by someone cheating at the lights. He's got away with it before, but this time he's ended up in hospital. If you cheat, you won't learn and then you'll fail the tests at the end of the year."

"No, I won't!" said George, stung. "Just this once, Charlie. I'll help you too—everybody does it sometimes."

The argument was getting heated and some other children joined in.

"Oh, yeah, George?" said Rahul. "But you 're always cheating. I've seen you shoplifting, too. You were caught red-handed last week. If that's your way of having fun, you'll end up in prison."

"Oh, shut up!" shouted George. "You're lying. Who's going to believe you, anyway?"

"We do!" shouted a chorus of voices.

"Rahul has never lied to us; that's why we believe him," put in Alice. "But you've lied so many times that we are not sure of anything you say any more."

"Good morning, everybody," said Mrs Mandy, walking to her desk. Everyone was quiet, but the teacher had heard what they were talking about. She put her books down and then looked at them all.

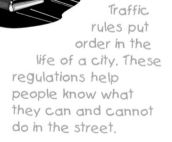

Corruption happens when rulers and politicians work at becoming rich instead of investing in the needs of the community.

Corruption is like cheating on a large scale.

Traffic rules put order in the life of a city. These regulations help people know what they can and cannot do in the street.

Countries become impoverished because of corruption.

"Let me tell you that cheating is like lying or stealing. It's dishonest—and people who are dishonest get used to taking short cuts. They don't want to make the effort to do things properly. But they also lose the respect of others and even of themselves. Think of crooked businessmen or corrupt politicians and how much they harm our society. Well, they were children once, weren't they? They probably started by cheating at school."

George felt embarrassed and kept his head down.

"Come over here, George," continued Mrs Mandy in a kindly voice. "Sit next to me. I can help you when you get stuck and that way you'll learn for yourself. You're an intelligent boy, and I'm sure that you can see that you won't gain much by cheating. If you make more effort, and get your homework done on time, you could do very well."

If you cheat or tell lies, people come to distrust you in other areas of life as well.

Al Capone was a famous criminal who ended up in jail.

As a young boy, he worked as the bodyguard of a thief. Then he started smuggling alcohol and that got him into more serious crime. Eventually he formed a powerful gang that recruited young men and trained them to be criminals.

The first American settlers believed in sharing and teamwork because they had to work hard to survive.

During their first summer, some of the group wanted to explore and swim in the rivers, leaving their companions to fell trees, build houses, cook and work the land. To put an end to this unfairness, their leader, Captain John Smith, established a rule: no work, no food. That soon solved the problem.

Traffic rules put order into the life of a city. These regulations help people know what they can and cannot do on the road.

Some youngsters become involved in petty crimes such as stealing, damaging public property, or just annoying people. They may do it because they are angry or because they think it normal to behave that way. Soon, they commit more serious offences, and then they find themselves with a criminal record.

Activities

1. Reread the text and answer

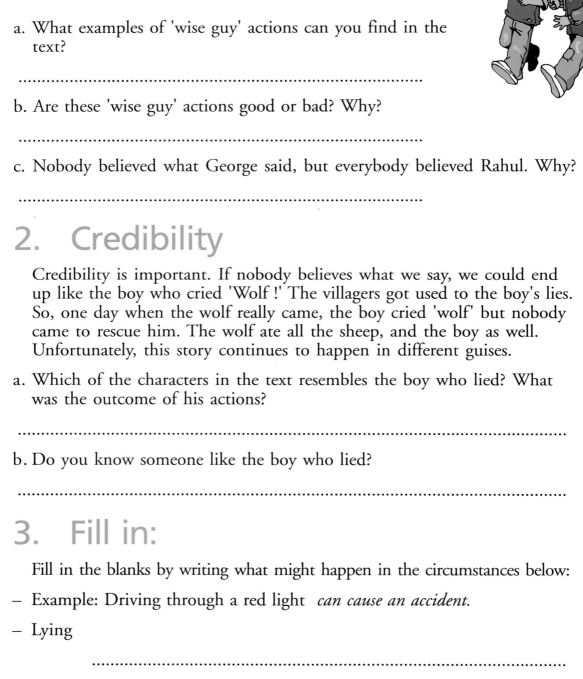

a. What examples of 'wise guy' actions can you find in the text?

....

b. Are these 'wise guy' actions good or bad? Why?

....

c. Nobody believed what George said, but everybody believed Rahul. Why?

....

2. Credibility

Credibility is important. If nobody believes what we say, we could end up like the boy who cried 'Wolf !' The villagers got used to the boy's lies. So, one day when the wolf really came, the boy cried 'wolf' but nobody came to rescue him. The wolf ate all the sheep, and the boy as well. Unfortunately, this story continues to happen in different guises.

a. Which of the characters in the text resembles the boy who lied? What was the outcome of his actions?

....

b. Do you know someone like the boy who lied?

....

3. Fill in:

Fill in the blanks by writing what might happen in the circumstances below:

– Example: Driving through a red light *can cause an accident.*

– Lying

....

– Cheating and not studying for the exams

....

– Stealing

....

– Trying to bribe a traffic warden in order to avoid a parking ticket

....

– Give other examples of 'being a wise guy' and the consequences.

....

4. Cheating affects us all

a. We know that cheats become bad professionals. What kind of a leader would someone who cheated in school become?

....

b. Leaders and politicians who cheat are corrupt. How does corruption affect a country?

....

c. Given that corruption makes a country poorer, what should we do to stop it?

....

d. What can we do to become honest and capable citizens?

....

Ask your parents or an adult at home what differences there are between the neighbourhood in which they lived as children and the neighbourhood where you live today.

....

....

....

....

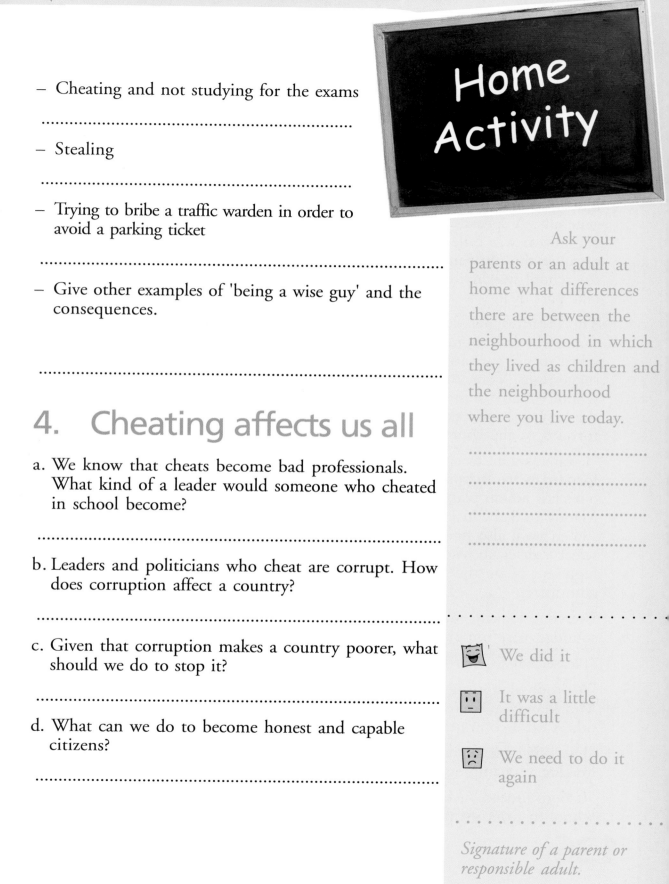 We did it

It was a little difficult

We need to do it again

Signature of a parent or responsible adult.

My Country

The local community decided that joint action was needed to combat the burglaries and improve the neighbourhood generally. A special committee was called to organise the campaign and the school was invited to take part in it.

The Headteacher decided that each class should be asked to put forward some suggestions. Then the whole school would vote to choose the best and send them forward to the committee.

"I want you all to come forward with proposals for our class action plan," Mrs Mandy told the Year 4. "Then we'll also have to select a delegate who can represent us on the committee."

Everyone looked puzzled. It sounded very important.

"Please, Miss, what is a proposal and what is a delegate?" asked Matthew.

"A proposal is a suggested plan of action to solve a particular problem," Mrs Mandy answered him, "and a delegate is a person who represents others on a committee or council."

"Does that mean that we're all taking part in the campaign?" asked Alice, looking very impressed.

"It does indeed," Mrs Mandy replied. "Mr Stevens wants everybody in the school to work on this. The neighbourhood belongs to us all, and we all need to look after it. Think of it this way: if we improve our neighbourhood, then we improve our town, and if we improve our town, we are helping to improve the whole country."

Mark's hand shot up. "Miss, can I be a delegate, please?" he asked. "I'll propose building a playground and—

"Wait a minute, Mark," Mrs Mandy stopped him. "I'm sure that you've all got good ideas but a delegate represents other people and so has to be chosen by them. You're all going to have a chance to make a proposal for helping the neighbourhood. Then we'll think who has the best ideas and vote for our delegate. Remember, though, to come up with solutions, and not just focus on the problems."

There are many ways to help your country; one way is by improving the place where you live.

"Miss, I think that people should be stopped from fly tipping their old sofas and things," said Charlie. "And there should be more litter bins in the parks, so that people don't chuck rubbish on the ground."

"It's more important that people obey the traffic rules, Miss!" put in Matthew.

Great changes are the result of many small

"Those are all good ideas," Mrs Mandy responded. "But if you are making a proposal, you will also have to think how it will work. How are you going to get people to stop fly tipping or follow the traffic rules better? Yes, Frankie?"

"Are we going to choose our delegate now, Miss?" Frankie asked. "Charlie, Mark and I all want to stand."

"Good for you. I was coming to that next," Mrs Mandy nodded approvingly. "But first I want each person to think of a proposal.

Neighbours can organise games, competitions, and other community activities.

Democracy:

"The government of the people, by the people, and for the people."

Abraham Lincoln

Then anyone who wants to stand will have a chance to come forward and describe his or her ideas to the class. Then we'll take a vote on whom we would like to be our elected representative. I'll ask you each to write down the name of the person you choose and the one who gets most votes will be elected."

To his surprise, Charlie found himself elected. He stood up.

"I know that I'm representing all of you," he said, "and I want to do it as well as I can."

"I wish all our politicians had that attitude," Alice remarked. "After all, their decisions affect us so much— our laws and everything."

"So they do, Alice. The people who govern us also decide how to spend our money. Unfortunately, the services we get back are often not as good as they should be," answered Mrs Mandy.

"Why don't politicians do a good job?" asked John.

"Well, you can't write them all off!" replied Mrs Mandy, laughing. "Governing anything is difficult, and running a local authority—that is government at the level of a town or a county—is difficult enough. Governing a whole

Florence Nightingale

Florence Nightingale (1820—1910) was an ordinary person who changed society. She came from a wealthy English family and was expected to marry, stay at home and have children. Nursing wasn't then a profession but a job done by poor, untrained women. Despite this, Florence wasn't put off—she even went to the Crimea to nurse British soldiers.

Florence's father had taught her as a child to present information using diagrams. Now she used statistics to persuade the government that many soldiers were dying unnecessarily from disease and that clean, well-managed hospitals would save lives. Imagine what she would have done with a computer!

country is very difficult indeed. There are good politicians and bad ones, and remember that it is easier to criticise than to do the work.

"When elected officials don't do a good job, it may be because the best candidates weren't chosen. People often vote for the wrong reasons. They support candidates who have instant appeal or make lots of attractive promises rather than the ones who are really capable. Sometimes ordinary citizens, like you and me, don't take enough interest in the community. And sometimes the best people don't stand. There are many reasons, John. What is certain is that good government depends upon everybody in the community being active and well informed. We also have to be brave enough to speak out.

"Democracy means the government of the people, for the people, and by the people."

"A Dutch Hero"

In Holland, there are many dams that protect the land from being flooded by the sea. Everybody keeps an eye on the dams because a small leak can have terrible, even fatal, consequences.

A young boy called Peter is a famous Dutch hero. One afternoon he was walking home when he noticed a leak. He decided to stick his finger in the hole to stop the water coming through. "I'll stay here until a passer-by sees me and gets help," he thought. But nobody came. Night fell. Although he was cold and exhausted, Peter continued to use his finger, and then his whole hand, to stop the flow of water.

Next day, Peter was found lying unconscious, his hand still in the dam. Everybody realised that he had saved the village.

DEMOCRACY

In greek **Demos** = PEOPLE

Cratia = GOVERNMENT

In a true democracy everybody participates.

1. Answer:

a. What does the word 'democracy' mean?

....

....

b. Why is democracy important, do you think?

....

....

c. Do you think that you can do something to improve your country? What?

....

....

....

d. What do you think citizens should do to make sure that they get all the services they need?

....

....

e. Do you need courage to be a good citizen? Why?

....

....

....

2. Write a paragraph to complete the idea

A neighbourhood is as orderly as the people who live there. What about a country?

....

....

....

3. Letter to your Local Authority:

Think about a problem in your area and what could be done about it. Then write a letter to the Local Authority.

Remember to:

• Describe the problem in detail.

• Tell them why it worries you.

• List some possible solutions.

Problem:

....

....

....

....

....

Re-read the text with your parents or an adult at home. Together, list the attitudes that promote democracy in your country.

....

....

....

....

 We did it

 It was a little difficult

We need to do it again

Signature of a parent or responsible adult.

Chapter 26

My Friends

"I'm so glad that you were elected!" said Matthew to Charlie as they walked out of the school gate. "Everybody likes you and you're always fair."

"Yeah—thanks Matt. But it's a responsibility and I'm a bit nervous. I hope I don't mess up," replied Charlie.

Matthew asked Charlie to go home with him to play on his playstation. Charlie wasn't crazy about computer games but liked Matthew, so he accepted. When they arrived, a group of children were waiting outside Matthew's door. He didn't look too pleased to see them.

"Hi, Matthew," said Peter. "We've come to play."

"Oh—OK, come in," Matthew replied unenthusiastically.

Charlie hadn't met Matthew's friends before. At first, they were all smiles, but then they started asking for things.

> Friendship: An affectionate relationship between two people, who trust and respect each other.

"Where are the crisps, Matt?" Steve demanded rudely. "Aren't you going to offer us a drink?"

"Sorry," said Matthew. "My mum's stocking up for my sister's birthday."

"Well, let's eat them anyway," said Peter, making for the kitchen. "We can hide the empty bags—come on! Your mum will never know."

A true friend feels sad when you suffer and cheerful when you're happy. A popular saying goes: 'Twice the happiness and half the pain when you share those feelings with a friend'.

Matthew hesitated. He looked at Charlie, who frowned and shook his head. Charlie by this time was feeling uneasy.

"Come on, Matt," Peter repeated, "or we'll never visit you again." By this time, Peter was already opening the cupboard doors. "We'll go to Dan's instead. He gives us loads of stuff, and his games are better than yours, too."

Charlie was angry. It wasn't his house, though, so he hesitated to interfere.

Matthew watched helplessly as the boys plundered his mum's larder.

Charlie was not enjoying himself, neither was Matthew. When the boys finally left, the house was a mess. Charlie helped Matthew tidy up as best he could.

Those boys aren't friends—they're just taking advantage of Matthew, thought Charlie. He was annoyed with the boys and annoyed with himself. "What would have happened if I had spoken up?" he thought.

Greeting each other by shaking the right hand is a custom that originated many centuries ago in Europe. It was done to show peace and that you were not carrying a weapon in your hand.

143

Activities

1. Answer:

a. What qualities do you look for in your friends?

....

b. How do you behave with your friends?

....

c. Sometimes being a good friend means making sacrifices. Have you ever experienced that? How?

....

Who you are, and not what you have, determines your value as a person. That's why people look each other in the eye: to see if the other is trustworthy.

2. Write:

Write about an event where you felt like Matthew or Charlie. Say how you felt and how you tackled the situation.

....

....

....

....

"ONE FOR ALL AND ALL FOR ONE"

This is the motto of the famous 'Three Musketeers', who protected a French King when he was a child. Their story inspired the French writer, Alexandre Dumas, to write about them. Athos, Porthos, Aramis and later D'Artagnan are examples of what it is to be a steadfast friend in peace and in danger.

144

3. Connect with a line:

Connect each word in the first column to a description in the second column.

Home Activity

Someone who is:	...is someone who:
loyal	• doesn't cheat or lie
a true friend	• feels the pain and sadness of others
open	• doesn't expect anything in return
compassionate	• doesn't put conditions on his/her friendship
honest	• you can always count on
unselfish	• is willing to listen

4. Define in your own words:

A friend is:

....

....

....

....

....

Chapter 27

My Team
of Friends

"What did your mother say, Matthew?" asked Charlie as they walked home next day.

"She was pretty angry," replied Matthew. "Charlie," he said suddenly. "What would you have done? Would you have just told them to go?"

"Put it like this, Matt," Charlie found himself saying. "I didn't like them. They pushed you about, they ate everything, and then they left. And today they didn't even say hello to you."

"But what am I going to do, Charlie?" asked Matthew desperately. "If I don't go along with them, they'll drop me for Dan."

"Well, let them! They're not real friends anyway."

"And you?" Matthew asked, looking at him. "Are you my friend?"

"I suppose I am. I don't like your kind of computer game, but I like playing football with you. And I've never felt embarrassed being with you, or anything like that."

Charlie was just finishing his homework later that afternoon when the doorbell rang.

"It's your friend Matthew," his mother called out to him. "He wants to join you and your friends for football."

Charlie put his books away quickly and looked at his watch. Good timing, he thought to himself. The others would be there just about now. He took Matthew out to the park with him and soon they were having a great game. Charlie was goalie, and Matthew played defence. He was very good.

"Charlie, you can ask your friend to play with us more often," said Eddie, when the game was over. "Are you coming back with me for tea now? What about you, Matthew? D'you want to come?"

Matthew felt pleased. Charlie's friends seemed so different. They treated him as one of them, even though he had had some problems and did not belong to their group.

Charlie was relieved that Matthew and his other friends were getting on well. He used to think that Matthew was a bit of a rough kid, but now he was realising that there was a lot more to him than that. He played football with real determination and he was always loyal to his team. He was also very open about his mistakes and keen to do better another time.

"Well, I said he was my friend," Charlie thought to himself. "Who knows … maybe he's even going to become a good one."

ESSENTIAL QUALITIES OF GROUPS OF FRIENDS

Openness

Generosity

Optimism

Sincerity

Team spirit

Responsibility

Spontaneity

Likeability

Effort

Loyalty

Enthusiasm

Courage

Loyalty is one of the noblest qualities. It means not doing something behind someone's back that you wouldn't do in front of that person. It means being consistent, respectful, and sincere. It means standing up for what is right.

147

Activities

1.   Answer

a. The first friendly gesture Charlie's friends made towards Matthew was to play football with him. What was the second gesture?

....

b. Why does Matthew find Charlie's group so different from his own?

....

c. What mattered more to Charlie's friends—what people thought about Matthew, or Matthew as a person and a possible friend?

....

d. What qualities mark out Charlie's friends as a group?

....

2.   Connect with a line ...

... the qualities of the group with the character/s in the lesson.

Openness
Generosity
Optimism   Charlie
Sincerity
Team spirit
Sense of responsibility
Spontaneity   Matthew
Likeability
Effort
Consideration
Loyalty   Charlie's friends
Enthusiasm
Courage

3. Write:

Write down some attitudes of a true friend.

a. *A true friend knows how to share.*

b. ....

c. ....

d. ....

e. ....

f. ....

Gratitude is important because it shows appreciation of others.

4.   Think and write:

What do you think might have happened to Matthew if he had remained with his group?

....

....

....

Friends HELP each other study

SHARE their love of sports

SUPPORT each other in difficult times

MAKE SURE they don't get into trouble

GET TOGETHER to laugh and have a good time

TALK about serious things.

"Loyal in spite of danger"

During World War II, two brothers fought in the same French battalion. One fell, wounded by a German bullet. His brother asked permission to take him from the battlefield. His commanding officer replied that it wasn't worth the risk since his brother would probably die anyway. The soldier kept asking until he was allowed to go.

When he found him, his dying brother said: "Tom, I knew that you would come... I knew it. You're a true brother." Tom was both sad and happy—he knew that he had eased his brother's suffering during the last moments of his life.

Being loyal is defending others when they are criticised and are not there to defend themselves.

149

Home Activity

Unit Self-Evaluation

Ask your parents or an adult at home to help you with the
Unit Evaluation.
Colour the shape that represents your performance in this
unit.

VERY GOOD　　　GOOD　　　FAIR

a) Why do you think that you deserve that grade?

....

....

b) What do you need to do to improve in the next unit?

....

....

c) How can your parents help you?

....

....

Signature of a parent or responsible adult.

UNIT VI

Seeing Teamwork in Nature

Objectives:

* To see nature as a great, interdependent unit.

* To learn about genetic inheritance and know how it affects life.

* To discover the marvels of nature.

Chapter 28

Part of Nature's Team

"Dad, tomorrow's a holiday. Can we go somewhere?" asked Alice as she climbed into bed.

"Well, what about a day in the country?" suggested her father. "Didn't you say that you are studying living things at school? It would be good for you to see for yourself some of the things you're reading about in class."

Alice was excited. Next day, she, Sam, and Teresa all got up early to make a picnic.

On the coach, Alice turned to her father, "You know, Dad? Mrs Warren says that nature is like a team—with all the different animals and plants working together and each being important. She told us that worms depend on roots, but that the roots benefit from the worms. In their own way even worms and roots are a team."

The journey seemed to go quickly as the children chatted happily about worms and other things. When they reached the nature reserve, they piled

noisily out of the coach, still laughing and chatting. Their dad called them together and, putting his finger to his mouth, he made them stop and listen. At first it all seemed very quiet, but then they heard a loud buzzing sound. It was coming from a beehive.

"Careful, Sam," said Dad. "Don't get too close. Bees sting—and it sounds like a swarm."

"Dad, did you know that bees help blossoms to turn into fruit?" asked Alice.

"So they do. But do you know what flowers give the bees in return?"

"Hmm, I used to know...," said Alice, scratching her head. "It's something they use for making honey."

"You're right—they do make honey out of it. It's called nectar and it's very sweet. The bees and insects fly from flower to flower looking for nectar but while they look they also pick up pollen in one flower and rub it off in another. This pollinates the flowers—you remember all about that, don't you? Blossoms have to be pollinated in order to produce the fruit which we eat. And if we then plant the seeds from the fruit, another tree will grow. And so you have a complete cycle.

Nature continues to renew itself in a wonderful cycle of life.

"Flowers are part of the cycle in another way, too. They give food to insects, then birds and other animals eat the insects, and then we eat some of the birds and animals. So, flowers are part of a big chain. Mrs Warren's right, Alice—nature is the world's biggest team," said her dad with a smile.

transport of pollen

anthers contain pollen

153

1. The food chain

Complete the following three chains by using the words beneath them:

Sea algae
Plankton (tiny organisms)
Small fish

Soil
Grass
Cows

Soil
Grass
Gazelles

. . . .

Words: Lions   Big Fish   Humans

2. Nature's team

As members of nature's team, we depend on the other members.
Nature's main players are in List A. List B shows some of our needs.
Choose a player in List A and link it to a need in List B.

A.	B.
Mammals	For heat and light
Birds	For growth of plants that provide fruits and vegetables
Insects	Give meat and milk proteins
Rain	Provides water for drinking and washing
Soil	Control the number of insects
Humans	Eat dead plant and animal matter
Sun	Take care of things, using their intelligence

3. Think and imagine:

Insects are sometimes annoying but we need them.

a. Why do we say that bees are good members of Nature's Team?

....

....

....

b. What would happen if there were no insects in the world to carry pollen between flowers?

....

....

....

c. What would happen if there were no insects in the world to eat dead plant and animal matter?

....

....

....

Humans can destroy this cycle through greed or carelessness.

Talk with your parents or an adult at home about how you can take care of the following members of Nature's Team.

Plants:

....

Soil:

....

Rivers:

....

Animals:

....

 We did it

 It was a little difficult

 We need to do it again

. . . .

Signature of a parent or responsible adult.

The Mystery of Genetic Inheritance

Alice and her family heard a tremendously loud noise. A herd of cows was being brought in for milking, and two of them had strayed towards them.

"Don't be scared!" said the farmer kindly. "Bossy's usually not dangerous, unless she has a young calf."

Alice came out from behind her dad, and asked if she could touch Bossy. "Come and I'll show you how. Bossy gives us lots of milk. She's a Holstein—Holsteins are easy to recognise with their black and white patches. And this brown cow is Gertrude. She's a Jersey. Isn't she pretty?"

"They look very different," said Alice. "Is Gertrude much younger?"

The farmer answered, "Aye, no. She'll always be small." He gave her a pat. "She eats less too. Cheap to keep, aren't you Gertrude? Now, she doesn't have Bossy's milk, not the quantity, but you should taste it. Can't beat it for cream. Best butter in the world comes from a Jersey."

"I don't like butter," piped up Samuel. "I like beef!"

The farmer laughed. "So you know beef comes from a cow, do you? Now if you want good beef, you need another breed. This is a dairy herd, for milk."

"How do you make a breed?" asked Alice. "I thought cows were just cows."

"Oh no, there are many types of cow. You breed them by choosing the father and the mother, so that you get the type of cow you want. There, I must be going. Come on now, Bossy," he called.

Alice and her family watched the farmer disappear after his cows. "What was he talking about, Dad?"

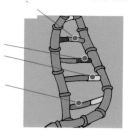

Alice asked. "How does choosing the father and mother create a breed?"

Millions of DNA genes determine the physical characteristics and the correct development of the whole person.

"You see, Alice, every animal inherits characteristics from its mother and its father. If you have a cow and a bull from a family of good milkers, their calf will also produce good milk. If you cross a milking cow with a beef bull, you may get a calf whose milk is less good than its mother's, but whose meat is better. Over time, if you choose your animals carefully, you create a family or breed of cows with the characteristics you want.

"Children also inherit characteristics from their mothers and their fathers. They are different from their parents—just as Bossy and Gertrude are from theirs—but at the same time they have things in common."

"Yes, but Dad, how does it happen?" Alice asked again.

"I know you've learnt at school that living beings are made up of cells," her dad replied. "Well, each cell has a control centre, or nucleus, hasn't it? Inside the nucleus there is an acid called DNA. And inside the DNA there are tiny tiny genes, and these genes contain the instructions which tell the cell how it is going to grow and behave. So you can imagine that cow over there as a whole team of cells each with its own set of instructions but all working together to make up the cow.

"Parents, whether they are animals or humans, pass some of their own characteristics on to their children through their DNA. That means that every cell of your body is marked with DNA related to me. Out here in the country, you can pretty much figure out which cow is the mother of which calf by seeing which ones look alike."

Human Genome Geneticists from around the world are working to build a 'map'—or a human genome—of all the human genes and what characteristic each gene determines.

My DNA is unique because I have a set of genes which is different from that of anyone else in the world.

My DNA identifies me and tells me where my father and mother's ancestors came from because it carries characteristics from all of them.

157

Alice responded, "Oh, then that's why dogs come in families of different shapes and sizes!"

"You're right," her dad answered. "And besides looking different, the different breeds have different talents. Some dogs are good hunters while others are good at racing. Some are fierce and make good guard dogs. Some know how to herd sheep—like German Shepherds—they are very intelligent and are often trained by the police for detecting drugs. Each breed of dogs has its own special qualities.

"It's a bit like that in human families too. I'm sure you've noticed that some families are athletic, or really bright, or artistic or musical. In part, this depends upon how the children are brought up, but a lot of it is inherited and comes from their DNA."

Mother + Father

Children

Genetic inheritance is the set of characteristics which we inherit. Half come from the mother and half from the father. That's why animals, plants and people look like their parents while at the same time they are unique.

The mule is a cross between a female horse and a male donkey. It inherits its agility from the horse and its strength from the donkey.

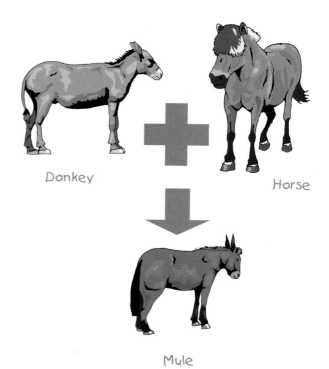

Donkey

Horse

Mule

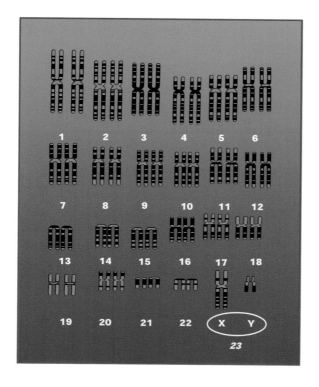

All humans get 23 chromosomes from their father and 23 from their mother to make a total of 46. Inside these chromosomes, there are millions of genes that determine how each girl or boy will be and grow.

159

1. Connect:

Connect with arrows the parents to their children.

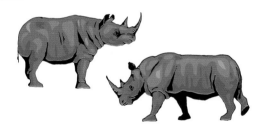

2. Find from the text:

Find from the text the information to complete the following sentences.

Each living organism has ....

Inside the DNA are the ...., that contain .... for each part of the body.

Humans also have .... in every .... of the body.

Every child .... some .... from his/her .... and others from his/her ....

3. Genetic inheritance

What do you think 'genetic inheritance' means?

....
....
....

Home Activity

a. Using a dictionary, look up the following two words:
Inheritance.....................
Genetic ....
Compare these words with the statement you wrote in Question 3.
b. Tell your parents or an adult at home what you learnt about genetic inheritance.
-Ask them what characteristics they think they inherited from each of their own parents.

. . . .

 We did it

 It was a little difficult

We need to do it again

. . . .

Signature of a parent or responsible adult.

Who Am I?

"Dad, is DNA the reason why I have hair like mum's and eyes like yours?" Alice asked over lunch the next day.

"You're very observant today!" her mum responded.

"Yes, you're right," replied her dad. "Even flowers—like animals and people—inherit their DNA from a combination of their father and mother. In almost every human cell there are 46 chromosomes, but there is an exception—the cells of a woman's ovum and a man's sperm have only half the number."

"Oh," said Alice, helping herself to a sandwich. "Why are they different?"

"Because," said her mum, "to make a baby, there must be an ovum from the mother, and a sperm from the father. They each contribute half the information about the child's characteristics, so they each have 23 chromosomes. Then, when the ovum and the sperm join together, they make up a new cell which has 46 chromosones all over again."

Alice stopped chewing to think about this. "So does the new cell belong to the mother or to the father?" she asked.

"Good question," her father replied. "What do you say?"

"Well," she replied slowly. "It can't belong to the mother, because it has half of the father's chromosones in it. And it can't belong to the father, because it has half of the mother's. Does it belong to the new baby?"

"Good girl!" replied her dad with a smile. "As soon as the father's sperm enters the mother's ovum, the two halves of information join together to make a completely new living being—the baby. You can think of the process like a puzzle where each parent provides half of the information. The information fits snugly together to make a new picture.

"The baby begins very small, of course. In fact, it is only one cell big. But all the biological information is there from the beginning which says how it's going to grow and develop. That's why children look a bit like their father and a bit like their mother."

"There are so many ovum genes in a woman and sperm genes in a man, that the combination of 23 and 23 chromosomes is close to infinite," added her mum. "The mixture of the two halves is never the same. That's why two siblings can look like each other, but they are never exactly the same."

Alice's father offered her another sandwich.

"Thanks," said Alice, eating hungrily. "So why are boys different from girls?"

"That is also decided by the chromosomes," her dad told her. "The twenty-third pair has a very special characteristic. It's made up of an X chromosome, which comes from the mother, and an X or a Y

163

chromosome, which comes from the father. If both parents give an X chromosome, the child will be a girl (XX). But, if the mother gives an X and the father gives a Y, then the child will be a boy (XY)."

"So does that mean that everything is decided by the genes inside the chromosomes?" Alice asked.

"Well, not everything," responded her dad. "After all, humans inherit much more than just physical traits from their parents. The love that parents give their children by taking good care of them is another way of transmitting characteristics. This is the love found in families. People are very different from animals—they need nurturing for many years. People have something inside that allows them to think and to love: it's called the spirit. Because of this spirit, bringing up children means more than just taking care of them and feeding them."

Alice's dad looked across at her mum.

"Yes," agreed her mother. "It also means helping them to grow emotionally and intellectually. And... did you know that even if a baby is physically perfect, it can't survive without love?"

"Two inheritances to make one person," thought Alice. "And in order to be able to grow, we need love!"

People inherit physical characteristics from their parents but they also inherit spiritual ones, too: the ability to think and to love.

When a group of people has similar features, we say that they belong to a certain race.

We are all humans with equal dignity, but we each have our own special qualities and customs.

Animals take care of their young until they are able to feed on their own. It takes some animals just days to learn, while others need weeks or months. Human children need their parents for many years.

1. Re-read the text ...

... and look for information to complete the sentences.

Like animals, plants also need a combination of .... from their father and from their ....

For a new .... to be born, it needs to have the ovum from the .... and a sperm from the................................. .

The two halves of genetic information join when the father's .... enters the mother's .... It's like a .... where each parent gives half of the information and when the pieces are joined, the puzzle is complete.

That's why children look partly like their .... and partly like their....................

The .... that parents give their children by taking good care of them is another way to .... characteristics.

2. Chose the correct option

The emotional characteristics are....................by love.

The physical characteristics are..........................from the parents.

3. Classify:

Classify the following characteristics as inherited or transmitted, by placing an 'I' or a 'T' by each one.

Home Activity

Characteristics	Genetics	Upbringing
Way of speaking		
Eye colour		
Good study habits		
Skin colour		
Respect		
Height		
Clothing style		
Values		
Hair colour		
Nose size		

Tell your parents or an adult at home the difference between inherited characteristics and transmitted characteristics. Use your own characteristics as examples.

Inherited characteristics:

....

Transmitted characteristics

....

 I did it

 It was a little difficult

 I need to do it again

Signature of a parent or responsible adult.

Chapter 31

Different But Equal

Alice was beginning to understand what her parents were telling her about genes, but she had a puzzle. How did her schoolmate Max fit in? He was the son of neighbours, but he didn't look like the rest of his family.

"Dad... you know Max? Why's he—you know—different?" she asked one day.

"He has a genetic problem," replied her dad. "Sometimes things go wrong inside the genes. It's as if some of the letters of the DNA message are repeated or unreadable. Then part of that person develops more slowly than normal—or some features may be altered."

"Max has Down's Syndrome," her mum said. "But have you noticed what a good boy he is? And he's always so cheerful, too!"

"But he makes me nervous," said Alice.

"Yes—because you think he's 'different'. But you shouldn't judge people by their appearances. Max is just like anyone else—he can do many things and achieve many goals. Also, look how affectionate and honest he is. It's too sad that other children think him different and don't want to be his friend—even exclude him from things—just because he's not quite like them. You know, that's called discrimination."

"I like Max, but..." Alice lowered her head, feeling a little ashamed.

"Don't feel bad," Dad said. "What you have to do now is learn how to treat him fairly. You can play together, learn many things, and just have a good time."

"Do you think that he wants me to be his friend, Dad?" asked Alice.

"I'm sure he does!" he responded energetically.

"Let's see if we can arrange for you to go over there one afternoon."

The following Saturday, Alice and Charlie went to Max's house and asked him if he would like to play. Max beamed at them and showed them all his favourite toys. He didn't speak very much but he smiled a lot.

When she got home, Alice told her mum that Max was so sweet. He had shared all his toys. But there were a lot of simple things which he seemed to be unable to do.

"Well, Alice, we are all are born with strengths and weaknesses," her mum commented. "As children, there are certain things that adults expect of you, like studying hard. Some children aren't able to study in the same way, but they still have tasks to perform in life. They too have to try to do those tasks as well as they can. It's up to everyone to try hard to become the very best person they can be. Max has to make a huge effort to do simple things, but his efforts are worth just as much as yours."

Alice had a lot to think about as she went up to her room: not only had she found a new friend—she had learnt something new about herself and about life!

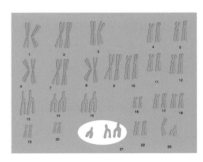

Down's Syndrome is a chromosomal or genetic disorder. Of the 23 pairs of chromosomes that make up each human cell, pair number 21 has 3 chromosomes instead of 2. Because of this, it's also called Trisomy 21 ('tri' stands for 3).

169

Activities

1. Think and answer:

a. Why do we sometimes feel uncomfortable with people who are 'different'? Is it because we don't know them?

....

b. How do you think that people like Max feel when others make them feel that they are 'different'?

....

c. What would you say to a child who said he/she was afraid to be Max's friend?

....

d. It is rude to stare at people who are different, but we shouldn't ignore them either. How should we treat people who are physically or mentally disabled?

....

People with Down's Syndrome or Trisomy 21 are born with a birth defect. It can make simple things very difficult for them to do.

But they are known for being cheerful and sincere.

They and their families deserve respect and help.

2. Complete the following:

When someone doesn't treat a 'different' person like everybody else, it's called

....

3. Order:

Order the events according to how they occurred in the text.

Home Activity

- ◯ Alice and Charlie went to visit Max.

- ◯ You have to understand how to treat Max fairly.

- ◯ Max has Down's Syndrome.

- ◯ He's always cheerful.

- ◯ Everyone should try to become the best person that they can be.

- ◯ That's called discrimination.

- ◯ Things go wrong with the genes.

- ◯ Some children don't want to know Max because he is different.

Talk to your parents, or an adult at home, about discrimination.
- Ask them how they feel about discrimination. Is it good or bad, and why?

....

....

Together, look for examples of discrimination.

....

....

"To be impaired in one's intelligence does not mean that one is any less in one's emotions, spirit, and soul."
Professor Jerome Lejeune, the scientist who discovered the genetic origin of Down's Syndrome

 We did it

 It was a little difficult

 We need to do it again

Signature of a parent or responsible adult.

Chapter 32

It's Great to Be Me!

Alice was greatly taken by the study of chromosomes. She liked knowing that all the cells in her body marked her out as belonging to her mother and father.

She also liked knowing that she was quite different from everybody else in the world.

And wasn't it strange that a small difference in one pair of chromosomes, the difference of having 'XX' and not 'XY', had decided that she was a girl and not a boy?

"What are you smiling to yourself about, Ali?" asked her friend Beth during break.

"What?... I don't know," Alice shrugged. "I was just thinking about how happy I am to be 'me'. I like being a girl and I'm really glad that one day I'm going to be a woman."

"Who wouldn't look forward to being a woman?" questioned Pearl, joining in.

"The boys!" responded Estelle.

"That's right!" exclaimed Beth. "Imagine if you told Ben and Frankie and Charlie that they were going to be women! They'd really freak out!"

As their teacher Mrs Grace approached them, Beth asked, "Miss, which is better, being a boy or being a girl? Some people say boys are more intelligent. Is that true?"

"Boys and girls are equally good and both are super-important," responded Mrs Grace. "Whether you are male or female is up to genetics. Did you know that generally males have larger brains?"

"What?" they all protested together.

"It's true," said Mrs Grace with a grin. "But women have more neurons. So, even if men have larger brains, it doesn't mean to say that they are more intelligent. You needn't believe everything you hear.

"I've never had any desire to be a man. I hope that you haven't either! We are all equally intelligent, but we have very different gifts. My husband and I are quite different from each other and I wouldn't want it any other way. We complement each other. And one day I hope I'll be a mother."

"Me too!" said Pearl.

"Well, to be a really good mum you need a good upbringing and a good education. The world needs both men and women. In quality and importance, we are equal. Everyone, both boys and girls, should always say: 'It's great to be me!'"

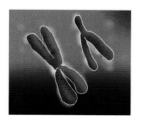

Genetically, every human is either male or female, depending on their chromosomes.

The chromosome pair #23 can be either XX or XY.

Brain differences between males and females

Males are often better at working with tools and solving mathematical and concentration problems.

They tend to be more focused in their work.

Females tend to be more fluent in speech than males because their brains are more integrated and the two sides are more connected.

This partly explains why women are believed to be more intuitive.

1.   Reflect

a. My DNA and me:

1. Do you have an XX or an XY chromosome in your DNA?.......................

2. Knowing that you have your own unique DNA, inherited from your parents and grandparents, and that you are also a product of your upbringing and your environment, do you believe that this sentence is true?

   "I should try to develop more as a person, and become more and more myself, to fulfil the mission that nature has given me."

   ....

b. We inherit many of our characteristics from DNA.

1. What characteristics have you inherited from your mother?

   ....

2. What characteristics have you inherited from your father?

   ....

Male characteristics are called 'masculine' and female characteristics are called 'feminine.'

3. Everybody has talents. What do you believe are your talents, or what talents would you like to develop as you get older?

   ....

c. Write down how you think you are today, and how you hope to be when you grow up.

   ....

2. Read...

Read this statement and mark T (true) or F (false) in the blank.

All people are identical ....

All people have dignity ....

Men and women are different, and they complement each other ....

A variety of talents is good ....

Important people are better ....

What we inherit from DNA determines our life ....

We inherit important characteristics through DNA ....

With your parents, or an adult at home, make one list with the traits you inherited from your parents or grandparents, and another list with the characteristics you've learn from them.

. . . .

. . . .

. . . .

. . . .

. . . .

A confident person feels happy and proud to be who he/she is.

Such a person acts the same way at home, with friends, and with everyone else.

Being self-confident will help others get to know and love us the way we are.

 We did it

 It was a little difficult

 We need to do it again

. . . .

Signature of a parent or responsible adult.

Unit Self-Evaluation

Complete the face by drawing the expression that represents your work in this unit.

Why do you think you deserve this facial expression?

....

....

....

What activities did you think were hard to do? Why?

....

....

....

Signature of a parent or responsible adult.

UNIT VII

Rights and Duties

Objectives:

* To know the basic rights and duties of all people, especially concerning health.

* To have a responsible attitude towards your own rights and duties.

Chapter 33

We All Have Rights

"I'm bothered about Max," Charlie confided to Alice one day. "Have you noticed how he always ends up having to sit in the last seat at the back of the bus? It's not right. It's not his fault that he's slow packing up. It's just the way he is with his Down's Syndrome."

"Yeah, you're right," Alice replied. "Those big children are not only quick. They always push to get on the bus first so they can sit in front! It's about time they gave way to Max. Just think how chuffed he'd be if he had a seat in front!"

They came up with a solution. With the help of several friends, they would hurry to get to the front of the queue and save a good seat for Max. Their plan worked, and it was their turn to feel chuffed seeing him beam and looking important.

But the bullies were cross. The following day, they decided to get there even earlier, and they ran and shoved the others to get to the front themselves. Then, Charlie, Alice and the others decided they would have to speak to them. They would explain that they

In-a-li-en-a-ble rights = fundamental rights that can't be taken away.

Some inalienable rights:

weren't being fair. Everyone was entitled to sit in the front of the bus and they should take turns.

"We get to sit in the front because we got here first!" the big children answered, laughing rudely.

That provoked a noisy argument.

Right to life

Mr Sullivan heard the shouting and came across to sort out the trouble. He called out over the racket:

"What's going on here? Since when does might make right? Everyone has the same rights, no matter how strong he or she may be!"

Right to freedom

The group was quickly silenced. Impressed by what Mr Sullivan had said, they shuffled quietly into an orderly queue. Max was ushered up to the front.

Mr Sullivan told them that he would be giving them a lesson on rights the next day.

Right to free expression

"And I want you to think about them beforehand. Tomorrow I'm going to ask you some questions. You need to understand that rights are the basis for justice in a civilised world!" he said sternly.

Next morning, everyone braced themselves.

Right to healthy growth and development

"Yesterday, some students were defending the rights of another student," began Mr Sullivan. "They thought that they were doing him a favour. In fact they were simply acting as civilised people who care about the rights of others. Rights are the basis for peace in the world, because all people are entitled to dignity and equal rights. If we don't respect these rights and make sure others respect them, a country can become abusive, which can lead to war. The quality of a nation can be measured by how the strong treat the weak!"

Right to safety

When Mr Sullivan had finished, the entire room became quiet as the students thought about everything he had said.

Did you know? ...
... That parental love and care is the most important basic right for our physical and mental health?

179

1. The right to life:

a. The right to life is the first and most important right. Why?

....

....

b. Why is it the basis of all other rights?

....

....

2. Think:

How do you think children benefit from the following human rights?

a. Adults' right to work.

....

b. The right to a trial before being convicted.

....

3. What does this mean?

a. "My rights end where the rights of others begin."

(For example, think about your right to express yourself.)

....

....

b. The right to equal opportunity.

....

4.   As a young person...

1. How could you help disabled people exercise their rights?

....

....

2. Under what circumstances do you think a child should be attended to before an adult?

....

....

Tell your parents or an adult at home everything you learnt about children's rights.

Find and attach a newspaper article which shows...

... a right being ignored.

What right is often ignored? Why?

....

....

A possible solution:

....

....

...a right being enforced.

What right is often enforced? Why?

....

....

Home Activity

We did it

It was a little difficult

We need to do it again

. . . .

Signature of a parent or responsible adult.

Chapter 34

We All Have Duties

The incident with Max and the group of bullies didn't end with Mr Sullivan's little talk. Now that the big children had been stopped from getting their own way, they were starting to complain that nobody was thinking about them. Mr Sullivan decided that it was time everybody got their heads together again.

"Tell me, lads, what's the problem?" Mr Sullivan asked the big children.

"Sir, it's not fair!" protested Rob, the biggest of them all. "Alice and Max and their friends now always get the best seats on the bus. We never get them any more."

"I'm glad to hear you talking about fairness and justice, Rob," Mr Sullivan replied. "Tell me, what do you think justice is?"

"Well... justice is... well... it's when I get my fair share," replied Rob.

"OK—and how do you know what is your fair share?" asked Mr Sullivan.

"Well... if I want something, and I'm the quickest or the biggest, and I win, then it's mine, right?" said Rob.

"That would be correct, Rob, if you were in a race," explained

Right to an education... an obligation to study.

Mr Sullivan. "But in real life it's not always the quickest, the strongest, or the cleverest who gets everything. Can you see that? In life, justice ensures that each person has the same opportunity. But the rights of each person are balanced by their duties. And one of those duties is to look after the rights of other people. Do you understand?"

"No, Sir. I think someone who can get more, should have more—stronger people have a right to a larger share," said Rob.

"But think for a moment, Rob," said Mr Sullivan. "If the strongest and fastest people in the world always won, in no time the world would become a very unfair place. Grown-ups are stronger than children. Would you be happy if they pushed you around all the time? Even when you grow up, you will find that there are people who are stronger and faster than you, or more intelligent. Do you want them to bully you?

"Justice is something different. Justice means that everybody has the same opportunity, provided that they also fulfil their duties."

All rights involve an obligation.

Right to good medical attention... an obligation to ensure hospitals are well maintained.

Right to safety... an obligation to respect and obey public and traffic laws.

Right to be respected.... an obligation to respect others.

1. Read and analyse the following statements:

a. When the traffic lights are green, everybody has the right to go through them without stopping. Everybody is entitled to this right because they also have the duty to stop when the lights are red. If you don't stop on red, you take away the right of the person who is going through green. What would happen if one person doesn't stop on red?

....

Why?

....

....

b. John and Peter received identical bicycles for Christmas. John always leaves his out in the rain, rides it over rough ground and never oils it. Peter always takes care of his bike. He dries it and oils it when it gets wet, and mends anything that breaks. Sometimes other children make fun of him because he takes such good care of his bike. After several months, who can enjoy his right to have a nice bike: John or Peter?

....

Why?

....

....

Rights and Duties = Care for things in order to be able to rely on them.

We can only rely on having rights if we defend the rights of others.

For example: Taking care of things we need and use means that we will continue to have the things we need. Saving our money is the only way to have enough for the things we want to buy.

c. Claire and Monica love to have pretty dresses for their holidays. Their grandmother gave them both some money for summer dresses. Claire bought 4 lengths of cotton material, worked every morning learning how to sew, and ended up making 2 dresses and 2 blouses.

Monica found cutting, tacking and sewing boring tasks, so she bought a dress with her money.

Who has the right to have more clothes: Claire or Monica? ....

Why?

....

....

d. During the holidays, Imran worked from 10 a.m. until 1 p.m. sweeping his uncle's small factory. He put most of his money in a savings account, and spent a little on toys.

After a few summers, does Imran have the right to have more money than his friends? ....

Why?

....

....

The right to be taken care of by adults means that we have a duty to obey them.

Home Activity

Tell your parents, or an adult at home, everything you have learnt about rights and duties.

Then, discuss what is meant by the following:

"When we don't fulfil our duties, someone loses their rights. If you don't have respect, someone loses their right to be respected."

Write your conclusions

....

....

 We did it

 It was a little difficult

 We need to do it again

. . . .

Signature of a parent or responsible adult.

Health:
A Right and a Duty

"Charlie's got the flu, so we can't go on our day trip!" announced Frankie to the group.

"Oh!" They were disappointed.

"Poor Charlie!" said Alice. "Let's go and visit him!"

They found Charlie at home in bed, his whole body aching.

"What's up, Charlie? How could this happen to you today of all days?" asked Alice.

"I think I caught something after football at the weekend. It started raining and I got soaked. Then, when we got home, I went for a bike ride with Stephen."

"Yes—you were really silly not changing into dry clothes," said Charlie's mum.

"Yeah," he agreed.

Healthy habit: "Everyone's body has its own natural defences. One person's defences are never the same as another's. That's why we should use our own cutlery and dishes for eating and drinking.

"And now look at you! You can't go out with your friends, and we're waiting to find out why your throat is so red," said his mum. "You're older now, and it's time you started taking better care of yourself. You know, if a throat infection gets really bad, it can affect the heart and kidneys—which eventually can even shorten your life!"

"Mum, don't exaggerate!" grumbled Charlie.

"I'm not exaggerating, Charlie. The body is a marvellous thing, and it has a tremendous ability to cure itself. But viruses and bacteria are the enemies of a healthy body. They can take advantage of any weaknesses in us and harm our health. So, we have to take good care of ourselves to help ward off illness."

Charlie started coughing...

"Cover your mouth, Charlie! That's why you have a tissue! Do you want to spread your germs to your friends?" Charlie's mum went on talking while she

It is unhealthy to share your ice cream—you might be carrying an infection that doesn't affect you but might affect your friend."

Vaccines guard our bodies against common illnesses. Years ago, people died from these illnesses because vaccines did not exist.

adjusted his pillow. She was in a really hectoring mood, probably because she was also a bit anxious. "Now, I think it would be best if your friends say good-bye before they catch the flu, too," she concluded.

Alice and her friends left, but they didn't feel the same without Charlie. Whether or not they had caught the flu, they had picked up Charlie's mum's anxious tone. Life wasn't always comfortable. It could even be dangerous. What illnesses might be awaiting them one day? Might they have a bad accident? What would they do if they did?

"One more week and it's the holidays," exclaimed Frankie. "Phew! No more school for a bit."

"School's not that bad," said Alice. "At least we all get on with each other nowadays. D'you remember that first class when Mr Sullivan said sport was the most important thing we were going to learn? And we wondered what he was talking about? Well, I reckon we really have learnt what it means to be a team!"

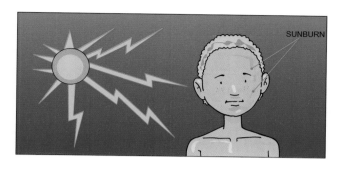
SUNBURN

Half the time you will ever spend in naked sunlight is likely to be while you are young. If you leave your skin exposed to hot sun, the surface layer literally burns. That's why it becomes red and blisters.

Sometimes the lower layers are also damaged, ageing the skin, and making you more vulnerable to skin cancer. Always try to play in the shade when the sun is hot. The sun's rays can still burn even when you're wet or there's a breeze. Put on a hat and long sleeves and remember to keep using high factor sun screen, especially if you're swimming. Its effectiveness doesn't double with the factor but only increases a small amount.

The Plague, or Black Death, was an epidemic that killed half the population of the UK during the fourteenth century.

In those days, people used to throw their rubbish into the street, so the towns became infested with rats. The rats had fleas that spread the Plague to humans. Today we know how important it is to keep our homes clean by removing rubbish promptly.

1.   Your opinion:

We are continually exposed to bad bacteria, but if we are strong, our bodies can resist them. However, if our body's defences are low—for instance if we have a cold or are under stress—our body loses some of its capacity to fight, and the bacteria can grow and multiply.

From the list below, tick the 4 most important health precautions:

- O Not coughing on others
- O Sunbathing
- O Not sharing cups and glasses
- O Eating a lot
- O Removing wet clothes promptly
- O Washing hands well before meals
- O Exercising

2.   Choose:

Many children used to die 100 years ago from infections and disease. Fortunately, today we know how to avoid most of these problems.

Choose from the list below the 4 important measures for a healthy childhood:

- O Vaccinations against infectious diseases
- O Not leaving the house
- O Keeping our neighbourhoods clean
- O Getting lots of sleep
- O Wearing a hat in the sun
- O Sunbathing
- O Putting rubbish in bags and making sure they are disposed of properly
- O Not swimming in contaminated water

3.   Order:

Acids form and attack our teeth when sugars and starches are left in our mouths. To keep teeth healthy we should brush them at least twice a day, and avoid eating between meals.

Number the following in order of importance:

○ Avoiding fizzy drinks
○ Washing teeth every morning and night
○ Eating sweets only after meals
○ Eating healthy snacks
○ Flossing between the teeth
○ Eating raw celery
○ Leaving half an hour between eating and brushing teeth
○ Going to the dentist every six months

4.   True and False

Bacteria and viruses are so small that they can only be seen with a microscope. We all have bacteria and also defences called antibodies, but they are difficult to see.

Imran says to Peter: "Have a lick of my lollipop! It's OK—I'm not sick."

Put "T" for True or "F" for False next to each phrase:

...... If Imran doesn't have a fever, he doesn't have bacteria.
...... Imran isn't sick because his defences are high, but he could have bad bacteria in his body.
...... If Peter's defences are low, he could be infected by Imran's bacteria.
...... Bacteria can't be seen.
...... Defences, or antibodies, can't be seen.
...... You shouldn't take risks that might cause infection.
...... There are still dangerous illnesses today.
...... Sharing a friend's glass or spoon is a nice, friendly thing to do.

Home Activity

With your parents or an adult at home, analyse the definition of health given by the World Health Organisation "Health is a state of complete physical, mental, and social well-being, and not merely the absence of disease or infirmity."

Note your conclusions:

....
....
....
....

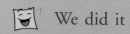 We did it

It was a little difficult

We need to do it again

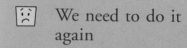

Signature of a parent or responsible adult.

Unit self-evaluation

Colour the part that represents your performance in this unit.

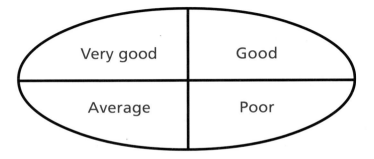

| Very good | Good |
| Average | Poor |

Why do you deserve that rating? What did you not accomplish?

....

....

....

....

....

Signature of a parent or responsible adult.